A Marx Dictionary

A Marx Dictionary

TERRELL CARVER

Barnes & Noble Books
Totowa, New Jersey

© Terrell Carver

First published 1987 by Polity Press, Cambridge, in association with
Basil Blackwell, Oxford.

Editorial Office:
Polity Press, Dales Brewery, Gwydir Street,
Cambridge CB1 2LJ, UK.

First published in the USA 1987 by
Barnes & Noble Books
81 Adams Drive, Totowa, New Jersey, 07512

ISBN: 0–389–20684–9

Library of Congress Cataloging-in-Publication Data
Carver, Terrell.
  A Marx dictionary.

  Bibliography: p.
  Includes index.
  1. Marx, Karl, 1818–1883 — Language —Glossaries, etc.
  2. Communism — Dictionaries. I. Title.
HX17.C37 1987   335.4′014   86–22172
ISBN 0–389–20684–9

Typeset by Dataset, St. Clements, Oxford
Printed in Great Britain by Page Bros, Norwich Ltd

For students and colleagues

Contents

Preface

This work is intended to help undergraduate students and other readers who are tackling Karl Marx's social theory as beginners. It incorporates my own approach to Marx and the lessons I have drawn from teaching his social theory to British and American students of different ages and backgrounds. While I hope that *A Marx Dictionary* may also interest more advanced students of Marx and the political and scholarly communities where his work is discussed, the book was not written specifically for such an audience. As it is from that audience that reviewers are usually drawn I shall try now to anticipate some of their criticisms and to recommend the book to its intended readership.

In *A Marx Dictionary* students will find an introductory essay on Marx's life and works. This is followed by my selection in alphabetical order of the sixteen major concepts that need careful explanation before his work can be grasped and criticized adequately. Through cross-referencing at appropriate points I aim to show the student how his concepts cohere. Cross-references are indicated by **bold-face** type the first time they appear in my introductory essay and in each entry in the dictionary section. It is possible to start with the introductory essay or with any entry in the dictionary section and then proceed along diverse logical paths until all the other entries have been covered. In that way the student can commence with an interest in any one aspect of Marx's theory, e.g. **alienation** or **exploitation** or **communism**, and work from there. Readers are advised to consult the Entry Finder and index, where many other terms used by Marx are keyed to dictionary entries, e.g. for 'constant capital' see **value**.

In presenting my interpretation of Marx's social theory I have limited references and quotations to works accessible to students and commonly assigned to beginners. And I have not introduced other interpretations from secondary literature into the text, because I prefer that students quarrel with Marx in the first instance and with me in the second. For those who prefer a more complicated scheme, there are suggested references to further reading at the end of each entry. Information about these books can be found in the bibliographical essay and bibliography following the dictionary section. A number of famous names in the secondary literature on Marx are absent from these reading lists because I have not found their works helpful in my teaching.

Friedrich Engels's role in interpreting Marx and establishing Marxist theory seems to me best dealt with once Marx's own work has been examined, and I have defended that position at length in my *Marx and Engels: The Intellectual Relationship* (Brighton: Wheatsheaf; Bloomington: Indiana University Press, 1983). To do otherwise is to risk begging questions about Marx's social theory that are profoundly important. Readers who wish to pursue the work of Engels and other Marxists might begin by consulting Tom Bottomore *et al.* (eds), *A Dictionary of Marxist Thought* (Oxford: Basil Blackwell; Cambridge, Mass.: Harvard University Press, 1983). Further reference from key words to short textual excerpts from Marx and Engels can be found in Gérard Bekerman, *Marx and Engels: A Conceptual Concordance*, trans. Terrell Carver (Oxford: Basil Blackwell, 1983).

Someone else would choose a different selection of concepts and write a different book about them. My intention is to start discussion and stimulate inquiry, so I do not presume to have said all that needs to be said about any aspect of Marx's thought. Rather I aim to make the student's first contact with Marx less forbidding than is often the case, without making Marx seem overly simple and dogmatic or giving the impression that this is the commentator's job. I have tried to make more use of Marx's masterpiece *Capital*, volume 1, than is usual in introductory works on social theory, and rather different use than is made of it in introductory economics when Marx is considered. Thus I hope to make *Capital* more accessible to the student, without neglecting the published and manuscript works of Marx that currently attract attention.

This is a book to start with, to move on from and (I hope) to come back to. I am grateful to Marianne Graves of Virginia Commonwealth University for her speedy, cheerful work on the typescript.   *Terrell Carver, Richmond, Virginia,*

Acknowledgements

Extracts from the following are reprinted by permission of Penguin Books Ltd, New Left Review, and Random House, Inc.:

Capital: A Critique of Political Economy, vol. 1, by Karl Marx, tr. Ben Fowkes. Copyright © 1976 by New Left Review.

Early Writings, by Karl Marx, tr. Gregor Benton and Rodney Livingstone, ed. Quintin Hoare. Copyright © 1975 by New Left Review.

Revolution of 1848 – Political Writings, vol. 1, by Karl Marx, ed. David Fernbach. Copyright © 1973 by New Left Review.

Karl Marx
Life and Works

Karl Marx's impact on politics has been overwhelming. But it has occurred through the medium of Marxism as interpreted and pursued by states, parties, leaders and followers all over the world. No more than a very few religious movements could challenge the position of Marxism as an influence on the goals towards which people strive and the judgements and activities that they use along the way.

The relation between founder and followers, between message and application, is just as vexed for Marxists as for adherents to the world's major religions. It is not surprising that Marxism has been interpreted as a religious or quasi-religious phenomenon, since texts and interpretation, orthodoxy and heresy, discipline and commitment, proselytization and exclusion have all been features of Marxist movements.

However, Marxism is not a movement that makes appeals to the supernatural. This is not to say that religious people and Marxists cannot communicate with each other (because they do), nor that Marxists never accommodate themselves to religious practices and views (because they have). Rather one of the most significant features of Marxism has been its appeal to **science** in some form or other as the validating factor that should convince us that the goals and political actions that Marxists propose are worth adopting.

Marxists have also attempted to undercut other major means of political persuasion with which we are familiar. These include particularistic views, such as nationalism and racism, as well as general appeals to natural rights and equal liberties. All of these are used to validate political programmes. Marxists argue that these approaches are deficient intellectually compared with the science that they recommend. This explains a good deal of the confidence so characteristic of adherents to Marxism, and the lack of common ground between it and other political movements which do not crucially depend on any view of science or may even reject it altogether.

The Marxist appeal to science may be powerful in principle, but how many Marxist movements owe their political success to pragmatic accommodations with nationalism? And conversely how close to real political activity are the highly theoretical debates about science for which Marxism is particularly noted? Science is not, so far, the political inspiration or intellectual activity that has decisively shaped the world of mass politics.

Yet there is no doubt that Marxists and Marx himself have contributed very substantially to social science as it is currently, albeit very imprecisely, defined and demarcated. Under social science I include anthropology, economics, political science, sociology, geography and archaeology. Literary studies, philosophy, history and aesthetics make use of material developed by these disciplines and overlap them. The terms of this list are not themselves important, because these disciplines do not share a common definition of science nor are they separated by agreed boundaries.

Marx is regarded as a founder of modern social science and a potent force within it. Indeed no other single figure in social science has had the intellectual impact that he has had. The political theory and practice of Marxists bears some relationship, however puzzling or controversial, to his thought. It is for those reasons that students are interested in Marx, and that his works are so extensively taught and used.

How has Marx's work stimulated social scientific theory and research? How did he attempt to use social science in politics, and what have been the consequences for Marxists? These are important questions to consider in a brief survey of his career. To answer them we must examine two issues very closely. One of these is the nature of his politics and the other is the nature of his works.

Marx was born into a Jewish family in Trier in the German Rhineland. In the Marx family liberal ideals and political compromise were familiar. But there was more compromise than idealism, as successive Prussian monarchs sought to contain the liberalism that they considered dangerous. Karl was born in 1818, just as the Rhineland passed from French rule under the relatively liberal Napoleonic code to rule by the king of Prussia.

In the Prussian kingdom 'the rights of man and the citizen' advocated by liberals were closely associated by loyal monarchists with the French Revolution and the ultimate political crimes of treason and regicide.

Under the Prussian administration of the Rhineland, Jews were no longer tolerated in the professions, where Christianity was made the rule. As careers were no longer freely open to talented individuals, Marx's father, a lawyer, had been obliged in 1816 to convert formally to Christianity, though he chose Lutheranism in a Roman Catholic community.

Although the Marx family do not seem to have been particularly concerned about religion of any kind, nor to have had strong feelings about their cultural heritage from European Jewry, the conversion marked a step backwards from the free-thinking rationalism that they valued. This outlook, associated with the Enlightenment in France, promoted critical scrutiny, scepticism and careful logic in considered opposition to mystical religious thought and to orthodoxies of faith. Revelation, arguments from authority and the weight of tradition were all rejected in favour of debate, persuasion, education and criticism.

When Marx's father accepted Christian orthodoxy and professed loyalty to a paternalistic ruler who enforced conformity, stifled criticism and claimed absolute powers, he opted for security. We cannot know all the feelings within the Marx family whilst Karl was at school, but it is recorded in correspondence that his father wanted him to be a lawyer and to enjoy the advantages of a secure professional livelihood. Karl never showed the slightest sign, however, of professing the loyalty to the law and to the Prussian monarchy that being a lawyer would necessitate.

Marx's time as a student at the universities of Bonn and Berlin from 1835 to 1841 was intellectually and personally exciting, a mixture of conventional and unconventional rebellion. He was transferred by his father from Bonn to Berlin because of duelling, debts and poor studies, but the stricter regime at Berlin failed to make a proper lawyer of Karl. Instead he associated himself with a crowd of philosophers, poets and student critics who promoted political liberalism and individual inquiry despite the pronouncements of university authorities. He wrote romantic poetry for a time, but soon progressed to the mainstream of philosophical debate at Berlin – the works of G. W. F. Hegel (1770–1831).

Later in life Marx was not keen to dwell on this period of philosophical debates and associations, because he wanted to distance himself from the 'Young Hegelians', as the politically liberal interpreters of Hegel called themselves. He particularly objected to their facile optimism that intellectual activity alone could move mountains. At the height of his career he wished to recommend himself to his readers as a conscientious scientist who analysed **capitalism**, the economic system of modern society. He contended that his theories were constructed with scrupulous regard for facts and logic and were not dependent on anything so insubstantial as a philosophy or philosophizing.

However, many commentators have asserted that this was the truly formative period in his life. Most argue that the scientific Marx only emerged after a crucial period of conflict within Hegelian and post-Hegelian philosophy, and that his concept of science cannot be understood without a reconstruction of this epic struggle.

There are two ways to present this conventional view. The first is that Marx's mature conception of science incorporated important ideas that arose from his contact with Hegelian philosophy, and that this defines a unique outlook. The second is that his mature conception of science required the rejection of his early criticisms of Hegel and indeed of any philosophy altogether, otherwise his mature works would not be scientific at all.

The latter view is by far the less successful, as it is difficult to imagine any work of social science, let alone Marx's, conforming to a science/philosophy dichotomy so strictly put. But the problem with the former conception is that it assumes a lengthy intellectual introduction to his work on capitalism that might have displeased him greatly, that might be daunting to contemporary students and that might shift the focus of his thought from social issues and action back to traditional problems in philosophy.

Perhaps Marx was mistaken in offering his works to the public without some prefatory consideration of the way that his premisses evolved. There is some evidence for this in his response to critics who, so he complained, had misunderstood the methods of inquiry and presentation that he employed. Yet his methodological corrections and rare comments on Hegel were brief and commonsensical, and they did not burden his readers with the 'Young Hegelian' debates or other philosophical issues in any detail. A reconstruction of Marx's early criticism of Hegelian philosophy has become standard even for novice students of his thought, but it is not clear to me that this is strictly necessary.

For our purposes in considering Marx's intellectual development, it is important to grasp that his student philosophizing was political, and not merely academic. He practised free-thinking criticism which praised Hegel's achievement in bringing history and politics into the realm of philosophy where the activities of real people and institutions were subject to assessment. Philosophical studies of a more abstract character, such as logic, metaphysics, theories of knowledge and perception etc., were thus made relevant to contemporary culture and politics as Hegel's system progressed.

Because of the ambiguities that Hegel loved, his work was subject to conservative and liberal interpretations, and Marx allied himself with the latter. To do so was to become involved in politics, not least because the university authorities were agents of a government that discouraged the very free-thinking criticism that liberals believed in and practised, perforce outside university premises.

The conservative warrant to discourage criticism derived from the most basic beliefs and values that they held. They identified truth with revealed religion as interpreted by the established churches. They supported philosophies that resolved awkward questions of faith or morals in ways that were compatible with orthodox Christianity. Toleration, scepticism and criticism were no virtues in conservative eyes. Rather they were vices to be stamped out, especially amongst intellectuals who might subvert the very training grounds of church functionaries and civil servants whose job it would be to oversee the thoughts and actions of the king's subjects at large. For most conservatives even moderate liberals were revolutionaries, even if they explicitly disavowed violence.

Marx's university philosophizing was political because the authorities saw it that way, and he was fully aware of this. He took his plans for a university job to the point of submitting a

Ph.D. dissertation to the University of Jena and obtaining his degree very promptly by post. It is clear that he intended to use an academic position to help liberalize the conservative Prussian regime. The liberal opposition in Prussia promoted rationalistic attacks on the established Christianity and the conservative version of Hegelian philosophy from which the king and Prussian authorities claimed their right to rule, including their supposed duty to regulate the religious beliefs and moral practice of the community. When the government cracked down on Marx's liberal friends who already had academic posts, he knew that he had to find another career. In 1842 he turned to journalism.

For Marx this was not a radical shift from philosophy and the academic life towards politics, since, as we have seen, his university period had been deeply political by the authorities' definition and by his own. Rather his work for the liberal newspaper *Rheinische Zeitung* marked a shift in political perspective from a strategy of elitism – by which intellectuals close to government service and the professions were to be radicalized – towards a broader strategy.

The *Rheinische Zeitung* was backed by businessmen in Cologne wanting a liberalization of government attitudes and practices that would favour the business community at the expense of the traditional beneficiaries of Prussian rule – feudal land-owners and nobility, the military forces, established churches. Rhenish business interests wanted increased middle-class participation in politics and therefore in government decision-making. They wanted to be heard and recognized through elected representatives, not patronized by hereditary rulers who burdened them with taxes and restricted their trading activities. The twenty-four-year-old Marx soon became editor, an indication of the difficulty of finding someone more experienced to run an organ that criticized the provincial government and defied the censor.

It is significant that Marx, in his articles, declined to stay within the political framework of which the newspaper's backers approved. He broadened his outlook to include a politics of social **class** that was unwelcome to liberals supporting the interests of the business community. For example he detailed the way that business interests and the monarchical **state** found common ground in revoking those customary rights in feudal law which benefitted peasants, such as the right to comb the forests for fallen wood to use as fuel. This legislation substituted statutory rights to exclusive private property for shared rights of use, so aristocratic and middle-class property-owners gained advantages at the expense of the peasantry. The rights of the poor to live modestly on the land were then superseded by economic necessity, and they were forced to seek paid employment anywhere it could be found. Marx also accused the state of ignoring the plight of wine-growing peasants who were the unwitting victims of natural and commercial forces. Under his editorship the *Rheinische Zeitung* grew increasingly provocative.

The possibilities for a mass politics that would involve the poor as well as benefit them directly were addressed in some of the very early literature of socialism and **communism** that came Marx's way whilst he was a journalist. One of his colleagues, Moses Hess (1812–75), advocated a **revolution** in politics and society and a determining political role in future for the industrial working classes of Europe, especially in Britain. Those ideas were obviously not welcome in the *Rheinische Zeitung*, which was forced to close in the spring of 1843 after censorship restrictions were imposed on it for publishing articles of a much less radical character.

The identification of communism with the current interests and political actions of the working class (or 'proletariat' in the French literature) was an unusually radical position. Yet it was such a view that Marx promoted immediately in his succeeding works of 1843 and 1844. These were published outside Prussia in small-circulation journals for radical intellectuals – for example, 'Letters from the *Franco-German Yearbooks*', *On the Jewish Question* and *A Contribution to the Critique of Hegel's 'Philosophy of Right'. Introduction* (in *Early Writings* 199–209, 212–41, 243–57). He identified himself with a communism that proposed the abolition of private property in land and industry and the achievement of this goal through a proletarian revolution.

Marx continued to upbraid German liberals who failed to raise the economic issue of social class and to grasp its fundamental relation to the contemporary state and to politics. The contrast between the liberal approach to ameliorating political conflicts through democratic representation and bargaining, and the thoroughgoing social and economic revolution that he associated with the communist movement, was a point that he developed assiduously.

By 1844 Marx's intellectual position with respect to politics was complicated and somewhat paradoxical. In addressing intellectual elites, he argued for mass politics. Though he accepted the need for social science, he advocated action by the academically uneducated proletariat. Though he admitted the progressive character of constitutional liberalism as opposed to the Prussian monarchy, he undermined the liberal vision of representative and responsible government by arguing that property-owners, not the poor, would be the real beneficiaries. Though he advocated communism, he eschewed speculation about a communist future and focused attention on contemporary class-divided societies.

Marx addressed elites on the inadequacies of elitism. He employed philosophical arguments to expose the inadequacy of philosophy. He used theoretical abstractions to explain the real world. He insisted on an economic framework for any consideration of political action. He theorized very abstractly about the very concrete character of contemporary social circumstances.

Marx has defied conventional forms of characterization, because the usual categories applied by biographers and commentators do not fit his activities. Accounts of his intellectual development which detail a supposed progression from the academic to the political, from philosophizing to action, from liberalism to revolution and from theoretical to practical activity misdescribe his early years. Marx did not become a Hegelian, a liberal or a communist in the course of his intellectual development. Rather he pushed Hegelians, liberals and communists towards an engagement with democratic politics. His relation to Hegelianism, liberalism and communism was always critical, and it is the concerns from which his criticisms flowed that mark an underlying unity in his career.

Marx's thought has an underlying unity, despite the diversity apparent in his works. This apparent diversity is largely explained by the different audiences for which he was writing and the various media he used. He wrote for a censored liberal newspaper, for uncensored journals published outside Prussia, for friends and associates in private correspondence, for legal publication and for himself. His audiences were middle-class newspaper readers, liberal and radical intellectuals and posterity.

The order in which his works were written is not perhaps as important as it has been made to appear in conventional accounts of his thought, because his choice of audience and medium was heavily conditioned by the personal and political circumstances surrounding him at any given time. While there were important intellectual achievements that occurred chronologically according to the texts we have available, a blanket assumption of chronological progress obscures the unity in the way his thought developed. This is because any given work does not necessarily record for the first time ideas that were never present earlier, or were previously denied or excluded.

Marx's early work developed from the free-thinking criticism cultivated amongst liberal intellectuals, an interest in poverty and social class, and the advocacy of broader participation in politics than the conservative state and even the liberal opposition would allow.

It was on those points that Marx found Friedrich Engels (1820–95) suspect at their first brief meeting in 1842 in the offices of the *Rheinische Zeitung*. Engels was an unofficial student at Berlin University whilst he fulfilled the compulsory military service that Marx had successfully avoided on grounds of poor health. Engels's associates were the student philosophers and critics whose views, however liberal, were disclaimed by Marx as amateurish. They seemed to Marx to overlook or distort the social question of poverty, the class analysis of society and the possibility of mass politics with which he identified himself. Engels was on his way to England, and whilst there he redeemed himself in Marx's eyes on just those issues.

Engels was two years younger than Marx, and came from a wealthy Protestant family of textile mill owners. They did not approve of free-thinkers and intellectuals, and Engels was marked for a career in the family business at sixteen. This proved alien to Friedrich's lively spirits and on moving away from home he worked in his spare time (and in office hours) writing poetry and literary criticism.

By 1842 Engels had dozens of published articles to his credit, many times more than Marx. Those works show a lively eye for social detail, a good deal of romantic enthusiasm for liberal ideas and some contact with the philosophical debates that were current in German politics. Engels supported the criticisms of the established churches and the Prussian state that liberals had generated, and he promoted their attack on the conservative reading of Hegel's work that was supposed to justify existing institutions and beliefs. Engels, too, met Moses Hess in Cologne, and found in his atheism and communism the logical conclusion to the problems in religion and politics that liberal criticism had exposed.

In England between 1842 and 1844 Engels made the sort of advance in economic research that Marx had barely envisaged. This was recorded in an outline for a critique of political economy, the economics of the time. Late in 1843 Engels sent his article to Marx, who immediately noted his enthusiasm in a conspectus that prefigured his own lifework.

Marx planned to look into the relationship between private property, trade and the **value** of goods in exchange. Two manuscript works of 1844 swiftly followed – *Excerpts from James Mill's 'Elements of Political Economy'* and *Economic and Philosophical Manuscripts* (in *Early Writings* 259–78, 280–400). The latter work is now widely read because in it Marx portrayed the **alienation** experienced by workers in modern industry. He also argued that **labour** would become genuinely fulfilling for everyone if capitalism were supplanted by communism and alienation abolished. Those early works were the beginning of a critical analysis of capitalism in which he planned to subject the works of established economists to scrutiny.

On returning to the Continent in late summer 1844, Engels met Marx and they agreed to collaborate on a pamphlet attacking 'Young Hegelian' liberals. This was the first of only three major collaborations that they undertook together during their careers.

By this time Marx had made a number of important decisions and choices. He had married his childhood friend Jenny von Westphalen in June 1843, rejected any idea of a civil service appointment and moved his household to Paris in the autumn to live near other radical *émigrés*. In Paris he expected to meet French communists involved with nascent trade unions and to work politically by smuggling into Prussia books and journals that could never be published there legally. Living expenses were henceforth covered in a very hand-to-mouth way, as he never worked steadily at any paying pursuit unless it was absolutely necessary. His critical work on the capitalist economy took first priority.

Marx's critique was expected to demonstrate conclusively that the problems of modern industrial society could never be solved on capitalist terms. He financed his work on it with money from his family and his wife's, and from loans, gifts and inheritances. Other sources were publishers and political friends. This made a very meagre life for his wife and children, and he later said that he regretted involving others in such circumstances. About the project and his own privations, though, there was never any real doubt.

Marx and Engels published *The Holy Family*, their first collaboration, in 1845. The bulk of it was written and signed by Marx, but the book bore the authorial names of 'Friedrich Engels and Karl Marx', probably because Engels was better known. As there was little mass politics in Prussia, the strategy Marx and Engels employed to spread their ideas and undermine their political rivals was indirect and somewhat rarified. They published highly intellectual satires and evidently expected liberal Hegelians to wilt under this scorn and fade away.

A 'Young Hegelian' reply to *The Holy Family* elicited a more constructive effort written up by the two in 1845 and 1846. This has survived in manuscript and was posthumously published as *The German Ideology*. While the manuscript contains disquisitions on social history and capitalism that resemble Engels's earlier works, the intellectual thrust of the book is probably Marx's, and Engels's role is generally taken to be that of amanuensis and contributor.

In *The German Ideology* the fundamental presuppositions and theories of the communist outlook were set down directly, rather than during the course of criticizing rival views. Those presuppositions were the existence of living individuals, their productive activity and the material world in which production took place. The history of human society was then conceptualized as the development of material production through different technological stages, the development of social relations appropriate to each stage and the development of intellectual and artistic artefacts characteristic of each **mode of production**.

Some of those intellectual artefacts were dismissed as **ideology**, Marx's term for ideas that purport to explain and justify the features of a given society, generally to the advantage of some groups or classes and to the disadvantage of others. But he did not describe his own presuppositions and deductions as ideology, even though they supported the needs and aspirations of proletarians at the expense of the business classes (or 'bourgeoisie'). Instead he referred to his own work as positive science arising from empirical premises and deductions. He believed that he had developed a distinctive science of human society, and he argued that it was superior to other conceptions, especially Hegelian ones which envisaged history as a progressive development of ideas such as 'rationality' and 'freedom'.

In Marx's view economic life in bourgeois or capitalist society, as he termed the modern world of commercial economies, was the product of a distinctive line of development from feudal society, which was quite unlike it. In mounting this argument he attempted to undercut claims by political economists and liberal politicians that the individualistic, competitive and acquisitive relations of modern times were unchanging features of human existence. The communist alternative to capitalism that he promoted thus became more plausible, in his view, once the existence of distinctively different human societies was accepted as historical fact.

The remainder of *The German Ideology* was devoted to further satires on 'Young Hegelians' that were all the more confident, once the new view of society and its history had been established to the authors' satisfaction. Unhappily for Marx and Engels, their publisher lost confidence in the project.

After Marx's death Engels published the eleven theses *Concerning Feuerbach* (in *Early Writings* 421–3), which Marx wrote during 1845. His few lines characterized the new outlook in philosophical terms as a non-traditional **materialism**.

The German Ideology and the theses *Concerning Feuerbach* were produced in Brussels. Marx had moved there after political pressure from Prussia caused the French government to issue an expulsion order. In freer and even more radical circumstances his political strategy broadened again. He turned away from merely reproving German intellectuals and concentrated instead on international correspondence committees, which were formed to publicize communism to industrial workers and thereby promote an anti-capitalist revolution.

Marx pursued the international dimension of his political work by attacking Pierre-Joseph Proudhon's *The Philosophy of Poverty*, published in 1846. Proudhon (1809–65) was a French radical and visionary reformer with an elite following amongst intellectuals and some reputation amongst French-speaking workers. His thought purported to be economic, philosophical, political and practical. It was therefore a credible rival to Marx's projected efforts, which were hardly underway.

In the French-language *The Poverty of Philosophy*, written by Marx alone and published in Paris and Brussels in 1847, he attempted a systematic rebuttal of Proudhon's economic theories and his methods of social analysis. Having read Adam Smith (1723–90), David Ricardo (1772–1823) and other classical political economists by this time, Marx found much of their work superior to Proudhon's analysis of value and to the Frenchman's view that economic life might be reformed to bring 'justice' to workers.

Marx dismissed as a muddle Proudhon's criticism of capitalist economic theory. Proudhon attempted to develop a socialist economics by applying Hegelian dialectic to political economy. This was roundly satirized by Marx, who considered the whole procedure arbitrary and far removed from fact. While facts must be conceptualized in categories, the application of a pseudo-Hegelian pattern of thesis/antithesis/synthesis to economic categories such as supply and demand merely disguised Proudhon's ignorance of real socio-economic phenomena that remained uninvestigated. Marx's conclusion was that Proudhon's work was a travesty of Hegel's philosophy and classical political economy.

Marx considered Proudhon's principles for the reorganization of society to be Utopian, far removed from practical communism. Those principles could never be realized, he objected, because they were fraught with logical contradictions and would in fact reproduce the class relations and inequalities of capitalist society, albeit in a slightly different form.

Moreover Marx charged that the political consciousness he thought important to founding a communist society was dictated to individuals by Proudhon in the form of intellectual principles. In Marx's view communist political consciousness arose for workers and others out of their actual struggles with capitalists. Communist theorists, such as Marx himself, merely helped to clarify political issues as they became apparent. It was from such a class struggle that he expected the new social relations of communism to emerge.

Marx aimed to contribute to this struggle by lecturing on the politically important but theoretically complicated topic 'wages' at the German workers' educational society in Brussels. He combined analysis of this economic category with his view of the class struggle and his explicit conclusions concerning the ultimate absurdity of capitalism. In those lectures he argued that the interests of workers and their employers were always in contradiction, that mere reform of the system, philanthropy or further economic growth did not alter this class-opposition and that competition between capitalist enterprises would lead to more and more destructive crises.

During this period the Brussels Correspondence Committee was absorbed into the newly founded Communist League, which was international in composition and secretive in character. This was to avoid the censorial and political repressions that openly communist activity in conservative countries would engender. In 1847 the League held two congresses in the relatively liberal atmosphere of London, and Marx and Engels were assigned to write a manifesto to guide the movement. Engels did two drafts from which the final document, their third and last important collaboration, was written up by Marx. The *Communist Manifesto* (in *Revolutions* 67–98) emerged from Marx's composition and editorial processes in January 1848.

While the manifesto for the communist party was written to represent a broad movement and to satisfy the League's committee, there are few traces of compromise in the work between Marx's views and any other line of thought. Other socialists and communists received some praise in the *Communist Manifesto* for raising the questions of class, property and industry. But 'feudal', 'petty-bourgeois', 'German' and 'conservative' socialists, in Marx's terminology, were castigated for their unworkable ideas about manufacture, property and the economic system. 'Utopian' socialists and their followers were taxed with standing apart from the working-class political movement as it grew up. Marx dismissed their principles and plans as mere personal inventions without practical value or theoretical justification.

The *Communist Manifesto* was published in German in London in early 1848 and had no significant influence on the Continental revolutions of that year. Those events began with the insurrection in February that overthrew King Louis Philippe (1773–1850) in Paris and established the Second Republic in France. A French translation of the *Communist Manifesto* appeared in midyear, and editions followed in other European languages, including English in 1850.

Marx was invited back to Paris by the republican provisional government. This was convenient, as he was expelled from Belgium by the royalist regime there which was fearful of a revolutionary uprising. In Paris he worked with *émigrés* about to return home to struggle for the liberalization of the various German states and principalities. Marx and Engels themselves went back to Cologne to write scores of articles (see *Revolutions* 112–318) for the *Neue Rheinische Zeitung*, the revived newspaper which they edited.

During this time the Communist League was dissolved, and Marx, through his articles, advocated the strategy for communists he had set out in the *Communist Manifesto*. His emphasis on mass action arising from the experiences of class struggle left no space for a distinctively communist leadership or even a separate party, which was specifically rejected as a strategy for communists. Communists were to be well-informed, leading members of existing parties, promoting the proletarian cause in ways appropriate to changing circumstances.

Marx advised the proletariat to fight alongside the bourgeoisie when it acted in a revolutionary way against absolute monarchy, feudal squirearchy and small property-holders. But he predicted that the proletariat would grow in numbers, in concentration, in unity and in conviction that only the violent overthrow of the bourgeoisie could fulfil their interests.

Marx observed that the social and political liberalization which the bourgeoisie must introduce to further its own interests could be supported by the proletariat and then used as weapons against their class-oppressors. These weapons were freedoms of the press and association, representative and responsible government and popular elections. Using these means communists were to instil into the working class the clear recognition that bourgeoisie and proletariat were irreconcilably antagonistic.

Communism would put an end to the **exploitation** of the proletariat by the bourgeoisie. This would happen through the conversion of capital, the property of a particular class, into social property. In that way factories and other productive resources would become a means to enrich the existence of the labourer rather than a way of requiring the labourer to exist merely for the good of the ruling bourgeois class. Communism would allow the appropriation of labour products by all, and no one would be subjugated at the workplace.

However, the *Communist Manifesto* set a political programme that was immediately democratic rather than distinctively communist. The first step in the revolution was to raise the proletariat to the position of ruling class by winning the battle of democracy. Indeed the proletarian movement was identified as a movement of the immense majority, in the interests of that majority, though in no country were industrial workers and their dependants as yet a majority of the population. Presumably the battle of democracy could include a battle of the ballot-box which the proletariat would enforce and defend, though Marx did not precisely say so.

Marx was perhaps deliberately vague about the institutional character of the battle of democracy, including the extent of suffrage and the role of women in politics, though both were matters of contemporary debate. The *Communist Manifesto* referred to democracy very loosely as proletarian supremacy and to women somewhat narrowly as ill-treated wage-workers under capitalism and objects of seduction by bourgeois males.

The *Communist Manifesto* offered a sharp yet narrow focus on the divergent interests of labourers and the propertied classes. The battle for democracy was primarily one of expropriating the kinds of private property – natural resources, raw materials, industrial plant – that allowed the bourgeoisie to employ proletarians and then reap the profits.

Marx suggested that a despotic attack on the conditions of bourgeois production was necessary and that this might cause temporary economic inefficiencies. Such a programme could include state-ownership of land, factories, banks, communications and transport; the equal liability of all to labour;

industrial armies for both agricultural and manufacturing industry, which would in any case be combined; free education for children that included an element of labour, though not exploitation.

More specifically the *Communist Manifesto* proposed a heavy progressive income tax and the abolition of inheritance as important measures to break down the concentrations of money and property which gave the bourgeoisie its power. The institution of egalitarian working arrangements, the nationalization of many enterprises and the imposition of limitations on the right to own productive resources were issues on which Marx offered positive guidance. Presumably he assumed that other features of social life could be adjusted satisfactorily within this 'dictatorship of the proletariat'.

No revolutionary movement of 1848 came close to implementing the programme of the *Communist Manifesto*, though there were brief experiments in Paris with reorganized industry and much discussion there and elsewhere of ideas like the ones Marx proposed. After the failure of the liberal revolutions on the Continent in 1849 Marx and Engels were forced to leave Prussia. Both took up residence in England, as did many other Continental refugees, and both remained there all the rest of their lives, except for brief periods when they travelled abroad for reasons of health, political activity or financial necessity.

During the 1850s and 1860s Engels worked as a businessman for the family firm, overseeing their interests in textile manufacturing and merchandising, chiefly in Manchester. His earnings were the Marx family's principal means of support until his retirement in 1869, when he settled some money on Marx so that he, his wife and three surviving daughters could be more independent.

Marx and his family lived penuriously in London where he had the advantage of the British Museum collections of theoretical and empirical works relating to the capitalist economic system, of which Britain was in any case the prime example. He also wrote an enormous amount of journalism on contemporary international politics for English- and German-language newspapers (see *Surveys* 250–353).

The first order of business for Marx and Engels after their arrival in England was to reflect on the failures of bourgeois revolutionaries and their proletarian compatriots in Germany and France. Engels wrote *Revolution and Counter-revolution in Germany*, first published in 1850 under Marx's name but now known to be Engels's work. Marx took the more dramatic events in France and offered a class-analysis of French politics that revealed a crucial ambiguity in the commitment of the bourgeois or middle classes to representative democracy. He did this in *The Class Struggles in France* published in 1850 (in *Surveys* 35–142); *The Eighteenth Brumaire of Louis Bonaparte* published in 1852 (in *Surveys* 143–249); and later *The Civil War in France* published in 1871 (in *First International* 187–236).

The historical generalizations of the *Communist Manifesto* became an agenda for the political problems considered by Marx in subsequent works, notably the series on France. In the *Communist Manifesto* capitalism was discussed in terms of the origin during the Middle Ages of a new class, the bourgeoisie. He gave an account of how individuals within it behaved, what changes in the economy and in political institutions it pursued and what long-term consequences were in store.

Marx traced the bourgeoisie to the burgesses or chartered burghers of medieval towns and ultimately to serfs who were freed from legal obligations to labour on the land or who were simply escapees from feudal estates. The bourgeoisie was identified with both trading and manufacturing agents who resisted the closed guilds and other restrictions of medieval Europe. They benefitted from the wealth and trading opportunities of the new markets and colonies that arose in the fifteenth and sixteenth centuries with the European exploration of the Americas, Africa and Asia. Opening the whole world to commerce on a vastly increased scale gave the European bourgeoisie the stimulus to create and meet rising demand by mechanizing industrial production still further and eventually introducing steam-power and large-scale industry in the late eighteenth and early nineteenth centuries. The industrial middle class, according to the *Communist Manifesto*, would be replaced in time by millionaires leading whole industrial armies.

As the bourgeoisie developed its power step-by-step within the economy, so its political power made corresponding advances which Marx noted in broad outline. From its position as a class oppressed by the feudal nobility, the bourgeoisie rose through the medieval commune, the independent city-state and the 'third estate' of contemporary monarchies. He foresaw a successful breakthrough to modern representative democracy. In that political form the bourgeoisie would guarantee for itself the freedom to develop and extend the industry and trade from which its wealth and power were derived.

Marx described the bourgeoisie as a revolutionary class in the *Communist Manifesto*, because in pursuing its industrial and political activities it attacked the hereditary hierarchies of feudalism and many other social institutions such as traditional family structures and the medieval professions. The bourgeoisie reduced religion, chivalry, sentiment and personal worth to egoistical calculation and to the cash nexus as it resisted and ultimately destroyed all the barriers in society to free trade and mechanized industry.

The laws and traditions of feudalism, so Marx wrote in the *Communist Manifesto*, became fetters on the activities of individuals whose mutual economic interests made them into a new class, the bourgeoisie. Eventually the productive forces of society, increasingly controlled by that class, would no longer be compatible with the complicated network of shared property rights and other commercial restrictions of feudal society. The political action of the revolutionary bourgeoisie would burst them asunder, as happened so spectacularly in the early years of the French Revolution. Private property in land and industry and free competition in trade constituted the outcome which he characterized as most suitable to bourgeois interests.

Ironically if political power were turned over to elected representatives in a democratic government bourgeois interests would be threatened. This was because the power of the bourgeoisie – in industry and in trade – was based on private property which the state could control through the legal system and if necessary by force of arms. The bourgeoisie supported representative democracy against the feudal system and absolute monarchies, but turned against it when there was political pressure to extend the franchise to the poorer classes.

Marx's emphasis on bourgeois revolution in the *Communist Manifesto* gave way to a focus on counter-revolution in *The Class Struggles in France* and *The Eighteenth Brumaire of Louis Bonaparte*. A turnabout in the attitude of the bourgeoisie to representative

democracy proved crucial in the events leading to the failure of
the Second Republic, founded during the revolution of 1848. In a
coup d'état of December 1851 Louis Bonaparte (1808–73)
overthrew the republic, installed himself as dictator and subsequently became Emperor Napoleon III. Bonaparte was a
great-nephew of the Emperor Napoleon (1769–1821), and Marx
pictured the younger adventurer as a somewhat comical but
undeniably successful swindler.

In Marx's account, the military dictatorship of Bonaparte was
preferred by the bourgeoisie to a democratic republic, because
they thought that a popularly elected government would be
more likely to order a redistribution of property counter to their
class interests. Such a state-directed reallocation could move
power and wealth away from industrial millionaires towards
other factions of the bourgeoisie. Yet the middle-class beneficiaries of such a process feared it might not be contained at that
point, and their wealth and resources would pass to the poor.
The very idea of working-class participation in politics was
enough to turn the bourgeoisie as a whole away from this
dangerous aspect of democracy and towards the supposed
security of authoritarian rule. The era of heroic bourgeois
revolutions, as in seventeenth-century England and eighteenth-
century France, was over. The enthusiasm of the bourgeoisie for
representative and responsible government had been soured by
fear of the proletariat, a new class with revolutionary designs on
capitalist property.

The *Communist Manifesto* presented proletarians or wage-
labourers as a class decisively different from the bourgeoisie,
because they had nothing on which to live except their labour.
The only way to live from labour was to sell it to industrialists on
terms dictated by the competition for jobs. Wage-levels were set
by industrialists at or below a bare subsistence, so that their
chances of increasing their capital would be all the greater, since
little of it would be paid out to the labour-force.

Proletarians, Marx declared for effect in the *Communist
Manifesto*, were without property, because they had no way of
gaining it except by working for capitalists. And they had no way
of increasing it beyond subsistence goods because of the free
market in labour, which was a commodity like any other. The
dynamics of capitalist competition within the market-place, as

he detailed this process, propelled small traders, handicraft workers and peasants into the proletariat as their spheres of economic activity became inefficient relative to mechanized production. Their property was purchased and their markets usurped by the industrialists, and they afterwards had to make their way as proletarians.

Out of the life-experience of proletarians grew economic struggles, contact amongst workers and the organization of the proletariat into a class. Eventually their interests would be pursued by proletarian political parties. The countervailing tendencies noted in the *Communist Manifesto* were the competition amongst workers themselves for jobs, national antagonisms which set workers against each other and the exploitation of one nation by another so that some workers were favoured at others' expense. All of those contrary factors were expected to give way, eventually, to proletarian solidarity.

Marx's generalizations in the *Communist Manifesto* also functioned as an agenda for the investigation of proletarian politics, much as his work on the bourgeoisie and the democratic republic was reflected in his lengthy analyses of middle-class politics in France. His investigations into the working class and its politics were undertaken in only rudimentary terms, mostly because there was simply less proletarian than bourgeois politics which he could consider.

In *The Eighteenth Brumaire of Louis Bonaparte* Marx wrote that proletarian revolutions of the nineteenth century were prone to failure, self-criticism, interruption and all manner of difficulties that stood in their way. Eventually the proletariat would reach a point, so he argued, at which further retreat would become impossible and the class as a whole would make the definitive revolutionary break with bourgeois rule.

According to Marx the classes of modern industrial society were subject to a dynamic located in the structure of capitalist industrial production that created not only class struggle but recurring economic crises of ever-increasing intensity. In his early outline for a critique of political economy Engels had focused on the inevitability of economic crises within a competitive system and the galvanizing effect this would have on the proletariat. Marx began defining this dynamic more precisely in the *Economic and Philosophical Manuscripts*, continued his work in

The Poverty of Philosophy and used that material in lectures at Brussels. Those lectures, now known as the short book *Wage Labour and Capital*, were published in 1849 in his *Neue Rheinische Zeitung* during the revolutionary struggles in Germany. That analysis of wages, prices and profits in simple language was one of his intended contributions to revolutionary politics, and the more obviously stirring *Communist Manifesto* was another.

The account of capitalist society Marx gave in the *Communist Manifesto* was not very theoretical in economic terms, possibly because he judged the Communist League and its constituency more receptive to a work that emphasized class, trade-union and party-political activities rather than the drier logic of his lectures *Wage Labour and Capital*. Or possibly the argument of the *Communist Manifesto* was placed at the level of class politics, historically understood, because Engels had taken that tack in his two drafts for the document. In any case the two approaches were not mutually exclusive, and indeed a very rudimentary economic analysis was incorporated within the historical and programmatic material developed by Marx in the *Communist Manifesto*. The posthumous publication of the *Grundrisse*, his notebooks from 1857 and 1858, has confirmed this consistent intertwining of class analysis and economic theory in his work.

Marx's intellectual drive was towards investigating the specific economic features of contemporary society, namely employment and property ownership, that determine social class. His conclusions led him to write a short autobiography and to sketch the guiding principles of his work in his 'Preface' to *A Contribution to the Critique of Political Economy* published in 1859 (in *Early Writings* 424–8). He generalized that the mode of production of material life conditions the social, political and intellectual life process in general.

Marx's analysis of the capitalist mode of production grew ever more specific in economic terms, and his grasp of contemporary and historical evidence bearing out his theoretical conclusions developed apace. His work in *Capital*, volume 1, published in 1867, on the **fetishism of commodities** and the exploitation of labour represented an analysis of the dynamic forces underlying the class politics of the *Communist Manifesto*, *The Class Struggles in France* and *The Eighteenth Brumaire of Louis Bonaparte*. In volume 1 of *Capital* Marx presented a fully developed critique of capitalist production, the economic system that in his opinion resulted from the activities of the bourgeoisie, oppressors of the working class.

In Marx's view the bourgeoisie conjured up the enormously productive machines and processes characteristic of modern industry, but produced a vast output of commodities by exploiting labour in mechanized production. Because workers competed for jobs they could be paid wages at or below subsistence as the bourgeoisie tried to maximize profits. Because of the race for profits, commodities supplied by competing producers tended to exceed the demand from consumers with money to buy them, causing a crisis of over-production. Producers then went bankrupt, factories became idle, workers were made redundant and depression ensued. Periodical crises were endemic and in his view more threatening each time to the entire structure of capitalist society as the disparity between unfulfilled needs and wasted resources became increasingly evident.

The theoretical case for worsening crises was developed by Marx in manuscripts of the early 1860s that were edited as *Capital*, volume 3, which surveyed the whole process of capitalist production. This work was published by Engels after Marx's death. In his manuscripts Marx developed a law concerning the rate of profit enjoyed by capitalists on their investments. He argued that the rate of profit would tend to decline, though he identified a number of countervailing tendencies. He concluded that capitalist economic activity would slump to a point of near disaster.

In the early 1870s Marx helped to produce a French translation of *Capital*, volume 1, and a second German edition of the work, somewhat revised, as well as manuscript material later edited by Engels as *Capital*, volume 2, on the circulation of capital within the economy. Marx suffered through the later 1870s with increasing ill-health, and he died of lung disease in 1883.

Although the communist movement has not been reinforced as straightforwardly as Marx expected by the economic crises of capitalism in the twentieth century, his focus on the way that capitalism upsets traditional economies has contributed enormously to revolutionary movements around the world. For Marx capitalist development was the realization of the economic definitions and deductions specified in the volumes of *Capital*, and he expected those theories to be of crucial interest in countries where the process of industrial development was newly introduced. Class conflict there would be all the sharper and all the more effective, because the contrast between new and old modes of production would be politically disruptive.

Marx speculated in the *Communist Manifesto* and elsewhere that the revolutionary overthrow of old regimes in non-industrial countries could act as a signal to the proletariat in capitalist nations. His perspective on revolution was national, but his vision of communism was international. He saw little prospect for isolated communist countries to fight successfully against the worldwide network of capitalist relations.

Marx was the theorist of the fully realized capitalist system portrayed in the volumes of *Capital*, but he has been most inspirational as a stimulus for revolution in countries where industrial development is only just underway or is a prospect for the future. Many critics have considered this a paradox, but, as we have seen, the paradox is only apparent.

Marx's belief in the irrationality of the capitalist system structured his non-authoritarian approach to proletarian politics. Indeed his own political role was consistent with this, since he advised and informed others within the framework of correspondence committees, international conferences and proletarian umbrella organizations like the International Working Men's Association, which he helped to found in London in 1864. He was not a party man in the conventional sense, and never sought to lead or to organize in any way other than as a wholeheartedly sympathetic intellectual.

Marx developed a critical perspective on capitalist society that situated it historically, focused on its class character and analysed the underlying economic interests. As he pursued that analysis, it became more abstractly theoretical and, he thought, more powerfully conclusive in indicating the features of production that make the opposing interests of bourgeoisie and proletariat in capitalist society a reality. His conclusions were published in versions for both specialist and popular audiences. In that way the intellectual and the worker were equally his audience and both were potential actors in a mass political movement.

Marx was never one for compromise with truth and principle merely to win allies or placate critics. His political tactic was always stern criticism of opposing views, coupled with strong intellectual persuasion in order to gain adherence to his own. Consequently he acquired the reputation within communist circles as a formidable thinker, but rather a bully when it came to disputes. He did not generally have the will to resolve them without undue disaffection and hard feelings.

While Marx was a political leader, he was not in practice a commander, since those communists persuaded by his analysis and views were left firmly to their own devices in carrying out even the actions that he deemed appropriate from time to time. Political organization was very largely left to others by Marx, who saw himself as a publicist making workers aware of the class struggle but not directing their efforts in a day-to-day manner.

Evidently Marx did not consider himself competent to lead a national workers' organization, secret or otherwise, and he refrained from meddling. Those in his circle did not press him to perform another role. At one level he was protecting, as best he could, the time he needed to undertake the critical analysis of capitalism which he thought would help to reshape human society throughout the world. At another he presupposed a radically democratic and egalitarian outlook that continually turned responsibility for decisions and action back on members of the working class.

For those reasons there is no detailed theory in Marx for effective political organization, merely a strategy of temporary alliances between workers and liberals against reactionaries, and a presumption that workers would eventually have to organize in order to fight against liberals. The liberal cause, in Marx's view, was ultimately a counter-revolutionary defence of capitalism. And there is no theory of political leadership in Marx beyond the rejection of conspiracy and the presumption that some form of representation would reconcile individual and collective interests within the proletariat.

Indeed it is unclear whether or not Marx envisaged as serious or potentially serious issues many of the problems that characteristically arise in parties that promote working-class interests. Internally those problems include organization, leadership and discipline. Externally they include many tactical problems, such as whether to participate in elections and governments, whether to seize power if the opportunity presents itself and whether to organize within or across existing barriers of nationality, culture, race and sex.

Marx's economic deductions concerning implacably opposed class interests and worsening crises in capitalism made it possible for him to shift the burden of political action away from theorizing by elites towards the life-experiences of proletarians. This allowed him to presume that proletarians would organize themselves as class and as a political party on the basis of clear, urgent economic priorities. Those shared interests would then undercut other differences, thus realizing a unity of theory and practice.

But whether Marx's economic deductions are correct is a question on which there is a large critical literature. If economic mechanisms are not as he portrayed them, then class politics could very well be more complex. The proletariat as a majority class would be less a fact that communists need only await and acknowledge and more a political coalition that would have to be forged. In that case communists would need a broader political agenda than the mainly economic one to which he largely confined himself. And they would need firmer views about organization and leadership during the revolutionary period than the non-authoritarian outlook espoused by Marx.

Marx's reticence on the subject of communism and the future organization of society was wholly in keeping with this approach to proletarian politics. Much of what he said about communism was precise only with repect to his vision of bourgeois society. Communists would abolish bourgeois property, bourgeois family, bourgeois education, bourgeois freedom, bourgeois culture, bourgeois law, bourgeois marriage, bourgeois morality and bourgeois rights. Communism was very briefly described in the *Communist Manifesto* as an association in which the free development of each is the condition for the free development of all. In the *Critique of the Gotha Programme* written by Marx in 1875 (in *First International* 339–59) he referred to it as a society whose motto is from each according to ability, to each according to need.

More substantively in *The Civil War in France* Marx evaluated as possible models for a communist society some of the representative institutions envisaged by participants in the insurrectionary Paris Commune of 1871. In that work he wrote approvingly of a structure of representative bodies, beginning at the village or workplace and rising to the national level, each body sending representatives to the next one higher up.

Proletarian representation was sharply distinguished by Marx from representation in bourgeois governments. Proletarian representatives would be strictly accountable for their decisions to their electors, who could suspend them instantly from office, and all officers would be paid at ordinary wages without any spurious trappings of authority.

That vision of the way to build communist society has set a high standard for Marxist movements. The ones in or near power have almost all been militarized as a matter of political necessity, a circumstance which Marx did not consider, even when he noted that the proletarian revolution would almost certainly be violent. For that reason there can be no clear verdict from him on the politics of twentieth-century Marxism.

From 1859 onwards Engels emerged as Marx's reviewer and popularizer, reproducing the class-perspective on politics and attempting to draw out the implications of the social science Marx was pursuing. As Marx's reviewer and as a contributor to the increasingly important press of the socialist parties which developed in Germany in the 1870s, Engels identified himself with Marx's views, as he understood them, and argued for their correctness.

Engels's works included *Anti-Dühring* published in 1878; *Socialism: Utopian and Scientific* published in 1880; and *Ludwig Feuerbach and the End of Classical German Philosophy* published in 1886. Those books were arguably more influential than any single work of Marx's in gaining adherents to the communist cause. The jointly written *Communist Manifesto* was perhaps an exception, but it is certain that Marx's formidable *Capital*, volume 1, and his simpler *Wage Labour and Capital* never played the role in revolutionary politics that he intended. Engels also published about two dozen introductions and prefaces to republished editions of Marx's works.

Adherents to the ideas put across by Engels, and those who believed that Marx's class analysis of politics and economic analysis of capitalist society were uniquely perspicacious, identified themselves as Marxists. In his own time Marx was not closely identified with any group of disciples, and he did not speak approvingly of a group of self-styled Marxists in France.

Marx commented that the novelty of his work lay in showing that social classes were historical products, that there was a class struggle in modern society leading to the dictatorship of the proletariat and that such a dictatorship was but a prelude to a classless or communist society. Engels endorsed this but made much more ambitious claims for the scope and significance of Marx's work.

In Engels's view Marx had founded a science that made a **dialectic**, derived from Hegel, compatible with a materialism that Engels saw in contemporary natural science such as physics and chemistry. He argued that Marx's scientific materialism was founded on dialectical laws applicable to all phenomena. Marx was said to have used those laws in his economic theory in order to reconcile historical evidence with logical presentation. Engels envisaged the further application of those laws in natural science, historical research and 'thought' or logic.

The dialectical and historical materialism outlined by Engels was further interpreted by Karl Kautsky (1854–1938), G. V. Plekhanov (1856–1918) and others. It remains a powerful force in contemporary Soviet philosophy and in most current accounts of Marxism. However, dialectical and historical materialism has a strongly interpretative, even academic bent. It seems to present communists with the need to reconcile their actions with the universal laws that govern everything, including social development.

By contrast Marx's own work offered a stimulus for the proletariat to overturn the specific economic laws by which he defined modern society as capitalist. His view of social scientific theory was that it should have a political effect when participants in the class struggle absorbed its message. Marx's view was brought into question by the laws of dialectical materialism, since Engels claimed they were explanations for behaviour which conforms to a law-governed necessity.

Shortly after Engels's death in 1895 doubts grew in the minds of some Marxists concerning the correctness of his interpretation of Marx's thought. The debate continues to the present day. It is certainly possible that some of what Engels said was inconsistent with Marx's writings and with the way that Marx envisaged his work affecting the movement for communism that he so strongly supported.

Marxism is a repository of different versions of what was said by Marx and by Engels. Later exponents and leaders such as V. I. Lenin (1870–1924), Rosa Luxemburg (1871–1919), Antonio Gramsci (1891–1937), J. V. Stalin (1879–1953), Mao Zedong (1893–1976) and many others, academic and party-political, have contributed. Some of their contributions consist in interpretations of Marx and Engels and of the relationship between the two. Other contributions are arguably original ideas on party organization, leadership and the politics and economics of building a communist society.

For social scientists Marx's legacy has been a research agenda that identifies the principal conflicts in society as those of social class. Most recently the term 'political economy' familiar to Marx has been revived to describe an interdisciplinary movement that inquires into connections between the economy, social class and politics. Marx conceptualized those connections as **base and superstructure**, a puzzling but very fruitful metaphor.

Marx's work has been uniquely stimulating in social science because he produced a general theory that linked politics to the economy through a concept of social class, and because he conceived of social scientific research as itself a political pursuit. His own attempts to use social science in politics were frustrated in his lifetime because his politics left so much to others and because the capitalist economy did not polarize class politics as dramatically as his economic analysis led him to expect.

Marx's work was narrowly focused on economic interests and deductions about capitalism. His politics was determinedly democratic and internationalist. Since his time Marxists have had to develop other social sciences and very different kinds of political activity to suit the circumstances of national and international politics in the twentieth century. For those reasons the relation between founder (if such he was) and followers (if so they are) will continue to vex Marxists and to preoccupy students of contemporary politics.

Table of Entries

Entry Finder

This Entry Finder comprises many of the terms and concepts associated with Marx's work. The reader is directed to the one entry in *A Marx Dictionary* in which a term is most easily approached. The cross-referencing within each entry then directs the reader to related aspects of Marx's theory. For complete page-references for these and other terms consult the index at the close of this volume.

absolute surplus-value *see*
  value
abstract or general labour *see*
  labour
accumulated labour *see* **labour**
accumulation of capital *see*
  capitalism
active labour *see* **labour**
alienated labour *see* **alienation**
alienation
ancient society *see* **mode of**
  production
average labour *see* **labour**
base and superstructure
bourgeois state *see* **state**
bourgeoisie *see* **class**
capital *see* **capitalism**
capitalism
capitalist *see* **capitalism**
class
commodity *see* **fetishism**
  of commodities
commodity fetishism *see*
  fetishism of commodities

common property *see*
  communism
communism
communist revolution *see*
  revolution
competition *see* **capitalism**
complex labour *see* **labour**
concrete labour *see* **labour**
consciousness *see* **base and**
  superstructure
constant capital *see* **value**
contradiction *see* **dialectic**
co-operation *see* **capitalism**
crisis *see* **value**
democracy *see* **state**
determinism *see* **base and**
  superstructure
dialectic
dictatorship of proletariat *see*
  state
division of labour *see*
  capitalism
economic crisis *see* **value**
economic foundation *see* **base**

The Dictionary

alienation

A term Marx uses to describe and evaluate the modern economy in which goods are produced for the market. He employs three German words generally rendered into English as 'alienation' (*Entfremdung*), 'estrangement' (*Entäusserung*) and the adjectives 'alien' or 'foreign' (*fremd*) to explain his conceptions. There does not seem to be any consistent distinction between 'alienation' and 'estrangement'.

The concept of alienation is most thoroughly rehearsed in Marx's early *Economic and Philosophical Manuscripts* of 1844, which were not published until 1932 and were not available in English until the late 1950s. Substantial reinterpretations of Marx were undertaken in the light of these writings.

Marx uses alienation to characterize an economic system presupposing greed, exchange, competition and private ownership of productive resources. In that system, he argues, money is used to **value** goods and to devalue people, because workers themselves become commodities bought and sold as **labour**. The devaluation of the human world, he writes, 'grows in direct proportion to the *increase in value* of the world of things' (*Early Writings* 323–4). Proletarian **revolution** becomes inevitable.

Four distinct aspects of alienation are detailed by Marx.

1 The objects produced by labourers come to oppose them as something alien, things independent of and opposed to their producers. Because workers have no control over products, which belong to employers or capitalists, and because workers have no control over productive resources, which also belong to these property owners, an alien world of objects confronts modern labourers as the autonomous power of capital.

2 Workers are alienated from the very activity of work, because labour has become a commodity sold to owners of

productive resources and carried out under their control. It
is done only under compulsion and has no intrinsic worth
for the workers themselves. With the introduction of
machine-labour, Marx argues, work more and more
mortifies the flesh of labourers and ruins their minds. It
becomes an activity of self-estrangement.

3 Work in the modern economy also estranges people from
productive labour itself, the vital activity of the human
species. Human beings, unlike animals, do not merge
directly with their activities. Their activities are objects of
will and consciousness and for that reason the character of
labour changes with each **mode of production** as economic progress takes place. In principle human beings are
'capable of producing according to the standards of every
species and of applying to each object its inherent standard
. . . the laws of beauty' (*Early Writings* 329). In practice
estranged labour turns this conscious life activity into a
mere means for existence. It alienates people from their own
bodies, from nature and from the essential human capacity
for free production beyond mere physical need.

4 As a consequence of being estranged from products, from
work and from the vital activity of the species, people are
also estranged from other people, in particular workers from
capitalists. The relation of workers to their own labour as a
mere commodity that must be sold creates 'the relation of
the capitalist – or whatever other word one chooses for the
master of labour – to that labour' (*Early Writings* 331).

For Marx the concept of alienation captures a set of economic
facts which he perceives and summarizes, but has not in 1844
attempted to document empirically. These facts are poor
working conditions in factories and de-skilling of labour as crafts
give way to manufacture. Workers also face unemployment and
penury when machinery replaces people. The wealth and power
of those who own capital increases, whilst that of workers
declines.

The concept of alienation also describes, in Marx's view, the
most basic feature of a system of private property. In principle
all other categories we use to conceptualize modern economic
relations, such as exchange, competition, money and capital, can

be deduced from it (*Early Writings* 324–34).

Only an alternative economic system, namely the **communism** Marx recommends, would abolish alienation. Indeed communism for Marx is non-alienated industrial society.

Towards the end of *Capital*, volume 1, of 1867, Marx employs the concept of alienation explicitly. As in the *Economic and Philosophical Manuscripts*, alienation appears after his critical examination of the crucial economic phenomena of modern society – wages, profit and rent – though in *Capital*, volume 1, his analysis opens with concepts that are even more abstract – the commodity, value and money. At an advanced, summary stage of the analysis in *Capital*, volume 1, he describes and evaluates the capitalist system as an embodiment of alienation in all four aspects.

1 Workers in capitalist production confront products as alien objects.
2 Workers are alienated from their own labour.
3 Workers become alienated from the intellectual potentialities of the labour process as scientific knowledge turns the human intellect into an instrument of torture.
4 Workers constantly produce wealth in the form of capital, an alien power which dominates and exploits them. Capitalists necessarily treat human labour as a mere commodity. People are therefore alienated from other people because capitalists accumulate wealth which is derived from the misery of workers (*Capital* 716, 798–9).

The four aspects of alienation also appear in earlier sections of *Capital*, volume 1, but they are implicit in the more specific vocabulary by which Marx characterizes **capitalism**.

1 The alienation of the worker from the products of labour, which confront the labourer as a powerful, alien, objective world, appears transformed as the theory of the **fetishism of commodities**.
2 Estrangement of the labourer from the labour process is detailed in Marx's theory of **exploitation**.
3 The alienation of people from labour, their vital activity as a species, figures in Marx's analysis and evaluation of the labour-process.

4 The estrangement of people from each other in society is reflected in the inevitably opposed **class** interests which Marx sees in the relation of workers to capitalists within the modern economy and **state**.

The recent attention paid to Marx's early manuscripts, in which commentators thought they discovered a humanistic, philosophical Marx at odds with the scientific economist of the mature works, reveals more about the presuppositions and preoccupations of commentators than it does about Marx's. In both early and late works he uses some terms that appear to modern readers to be philosophical and some that appear to be economic. But with respect to his analysis of society the distinction is invalid, as his thought does not conform to the terms of either modern academic discipline. In his work Marx aims to produce a critical **science** of society, combining description with evaluation and using concepts and methods from a wide range of sources.

FURTHER READING

A Marx Dictionary

capitalism	**mode of production**
class	**revolution**
communism	**science**
exploitation	**state**
fetishism of commodities	**value**
labour	

Marx's writings
Capital, especially pp. 716, 798–9
Early Writings 'Economic and Philosophical Manuscripts', especially pp. 322–34

Secondary sources
Avineri (1970), especially chapter 4
Maguire (1972), especially chapters 3–4
Mészáros (1972), especially chapter III and parts II–III
Ollman (1976), especially part III
Walton and Gamble (1972), especially chapters 1–2
Wood (1981), especially part 1

base and superstructure

A metaphor Marx uses in explaining the fundamentals of his social theory. 'Base' (in German *Basis*) is sometimes translated as 'basis' or, more commonly, 'foundation'. The metaphor occurs in what is probably the most important and puzzling passage in all his works. In his 1859 'Preface' to *A Contribution to the Critique of Political Economy* he advises his reader of 'the general conclusion at which I arrived and which, once reached, became the guiding principle of my studies'. These are studies of 'social production' where people further their existence in society by entering 'relations of production'. 'The totality of these relations of production', he comments, 'constitutes the economic structure of society'. He calls the economic structure of society a 'real foundation' on which 'arises a legal and political superstructure' (*Early Writings* 425).

By using the base/superstructure metaphor Marx suggests a distinction, but does not specify precisely what the distinction encompasses. Exactly which social activities and institutions belong to the base and which to the superstructure are questions that he never addresses definitively. Nor is it made clear whether different aspects of any one activity or institution may be conceptualized as belonging to the base, and other aspects to the superstructure.

The commonplace interpretation of the metaphor – that the economic base is somehow material as opposed to a super-structure of ideas – does not fit Marx's view. He uses the concept of the base to refer to the purposive behaviour that constitutes economic activity. In economic activity people employ the tools and machines which he calls the 'forces of production', and to do this people must use ideas. The legal and political super-structure, while referring to ideas and beliefs, covers activities in society that take on a material form. He mentions the 'legal, political, religious, artistic, or philosophic – in short, ideological forms' of consciousness that exist in society and sometimes figure in social conflict. On occasion this is so indubitably material that he refers to such conflict as a 'fight' (*Early Writings* 425–6).

When Marx writes that the superstructure arises from a real foundation he suggests a relationship between them. He attempts to explain it in a summary sentence which virtually encapsulates his entire social theory. 'The **mode of production** of material life conditions the general process of social, political, and intellectual life' (*Early Writings* 425). But the terms 'mode of production' and 'process of life' are never strictly defined and their relation never clarified. Nor is the verb 'conditions' defined and explained.

Is Marx implying that superstructural phenomena can be traced causally to the base? Or is he saying that they can be explained through their functional relationship to it? Commentators have argued for those different interpretations, but they have been seriously criticized for unconvincing definitions of 'base' and 'superstructure', 'cause' and 'function'. Moreover when commentators apply those interpretations of Marx's base and superstructure metaphor to explaining historical events they produce uneven results. Indeed whether Marx's base and superstructure metaphor constitutes a scientific law or 'determinism' which a counter-example could invalidate, or whether it is some looser kind of generalization, is a very serious question any interpreter must face.

Perhaps Marx's metaphor of base and superstructure is best understood as a guide to social research, leading the researcher from base to superstructure, that is, from relations of production to the **state**. This is in line with Marx's general claim that society has a real foundation in economic activity from which arises a superstructure of legal, political and cultural beliefs and institutions.

The base/superstructure metaphor has been characterized as the core of the 'materialist interpretation of history' or 'historical **materialism**'. Neither phrase was used by Marx. What he says about the economic base underlies his theory of **class**, and his comments on superstructure contribute to his theory of **ideology**. Evidently the distinctions and difficulties implied in his loosely formulated guiding principle were of less importance to him than the detailed results of his critical study of **capitalism**, the work he was briefly introducing in the 'Preface' to *A Contribution to the Critique of Political Economy* where the metaphor most famously occurs.

FURTHER READING

A Marx Dictionary

capitalism

class

ideology

materialism

mode of production

state

Marx's writings

Capital, especially pp. 175n, 285–6, 425, 432, 479, 493–4n, 504

Early Writings, 'Preface' (1859), pp. 425–6

Secondary sources

Carver (1982), especially chapter 3

Cohen (1978), especially chapters III, VIII

Rader (1979), especially chapter 1

Shaw (1978), especially chapter 1

Suchting (1983), especially chapter 16

Wood (1981), especially chapters V, VII

capitalism

A term Marx uses to denote the economic system in which production is for the market. In his view a new **class**, the bourgeoisie, expanded trade and increased production, starting in Europe in the early Middle Ages. To do this it changed the terms on which people applied their **labour** to production and so created the proletariat or working class. In the *Communist Manifesto* of 1848 he refers to 'the bourgeoisie, i.e. capital' (*Revolutions* 73). And in *Capital*, volume 1, of 1867, he refers to the capitalist **mode of production** and to modern bourgeois society more or less interchangeably. In that form of society useful goods and services become an 'immense collection of commodities' (*Capital* 125).

In *Capital*, volume 1, the opening of Marx's critical analysis of capitalism, the reader is directed in the first chapter towards the **fetishism of commodities**. Since wealth in capitalist societies takes the form of commodities, Marx begins with the individual commodity as the relevant unit for analysis. In his discussion he uses a twofold concept of **value** – use-value and exchange-value – to explain the concept or 'form' of the commodity. In that way he outlines the distinctive, socially held assumptions that in capitalist society make the products of labour into commodities. Under **communism**, as he envisages it, those assumptions would be radically altered.

Marx is well aware that his careful groundwork on the commodity, its value, the money-commodity and the market will seem a slow road to the reader expecting immediate revelations about capital and capitalism. Indeed most commentaries on his work treat the theories of value, **exploitation**, **alienation**, **revolution** and **state** as a cumulative theory of capitalist society, without addressing his specific propositions about capitalism as a contemporary system. Those specific propositions form a conceptual reconstruction which he uses to interpret historical and contemporary evidence. The evidence he cites is designed to make his conceptual reconstruction of capitalism plausible and persuasive.

Trade, for Marx, is the historic presupposition of capital. 'The discovery of America, the rounding of the Cape . . . the East Indian and Chinese markets . . . gave to commerce, to navigation, to industry, an impulse never before known', he comments in the *Communist Manifesto* (*Revolutions* 68). 'World trade and the world market date from the sixteenth century', he writes in *Capital*, volume 1, and 'from then on the modern history of capital starts to unfold'. Conceptually trade is the circulation of commodities that proceeds from their very conditions of production. Commodities are useful things produced *for exchange* (*Capital* 166, 247).

From the exchange of commodities arises money, or as Marx terms it, the money-commodity. As products of labour are transformed into commodities, so at the same rate is one particular commodity transformed into money, the universal equivalent in which the values of all other commodities can be represented. Which commodity performs this function first is a matter of mere accident, he suggests, but as exchange develops, the money-form of the commodity is attached either to the most important articles of exchange, or to the article which is the chief element of alienable wealth within an economy. Eventually precious metals serve this function, because they are homogeneous in character, easily divisible and relatively costly per unit of weight in terms of human labour, so that small quantities by weight represent sizeable quantities of value.

Marx does not recognize the full validity of the term capital in ancient societies even though there was some trade in commodities and some use of money. While the circulation of commodities is the starting-point of capital, this circulation itself has two phases. The second of these is seized on by Marx as historically and analytically defining for capital.

The first phase of the circulation of commodities is merely the exchange of commodities for money in order to buy and consume other commodities – selling in order to buy. It is on that basis, and only with the development of stable currencies, banks, accounting systems and other early modern financial institutions, that the second phase of circulation can be established.

This is the circulation of the money-commodity in exchange for other commodities, which are then re-sold for money itself. This is buying in order to sell. The determining purpose of that circulation is therefore the acquisition of exchange-value rather than consumption to satisfy needs.

Exchange-value, being a purely quantitative relation in Marx's view, is in principle limitless. Analytically he sees capital as the circulation of the money-commodity, the exchange of money for money, as in the accumulation of interest or money-capital. This exchange is absurd, he argues, unless the final sum is larger than the initial one by an increment or surplus-value. Conceptually the function of a purely quantitative measure such as exchange-value is 'to approach, by quantitative increase, as near as possible to absolute wealth'. The movement of capital, he concludes, is therefore limitless, and the aim of the capitalist is the 'ceaseless augmentation of value . . . by means of throwing his money again and again into circulation'. Capital is therefore money in a special form of circulation with commodities, buying in order to sell dearer, a form easily observed in merchants' capital, where money is exchanged for commodities but returns to its original owner with profit. But it is also common to industrial capital where, he argues, the new values that make profits possible are created by the application of human labour to raw materials (*Capital* 248–57).

Industrial production is crucial to Marx's view of capital and capitalism, because he argues that new values cannot arise out of the simple circulation of commodities and money, whether the circulation is one where equivalents in value are exchanged, or where there is an exchange of non-equivalents. 'The formation of surplus-value', he writes, and 'therefore the transformation of money into capital', can be explained neither on the assumption that commodities are sold above their value, nor on the assumption that they are bought at less than their value. He argues that the sum of the values in circulation cannot be increased by any change in their distribution and that the 'capitalist class of a given country, taken as a whole, cannot defraud itself'. Any 'cheating' by one trader at the expense of another will be cancelled out within the system, either by a general rise in values as equivalents are exchanged (hence no overall increase in value) or by a redistribution of value as profits and losses which equalize themselves amongst all traders (*Capital* 263–7).

For Marx the purchase of human labour-power by the individual capitalist is the only way of creating new values (the surplus-value from which profits uniquely derive), because labour-power is the only commodity which is a source of more value than it has already incorporated within itself. Past labour in products that form the means of subsistence of the labourer, and the amount of labour that can subsequently be performed by a living worker, are not necessarily equal. The labour-output of any worker can exceed the reproduction cost of the labourer in value-terms by a very large margin. Because capitalists own the means of production, they are in a position to offer money-wages to workers, whilst retaining an ownership right over all the commodities that emerge from the labour-process.

Thus the stage is set for Marx's analysis of modern industrial society. Without the stimulus of capital, highly productive industries would not have developed. Indeed for Marx capital and the stimulus to revolutionize production by putting it on an industrial footing are basically the same process.

Marx has difficulty imagining a transition from feudal to industrial society on a non-capitalist basis, though he does not rule it out entirely. And his concept of capitalism requires the development of modern industry as a matter of definition, because for him modern industrial production is in essence a way of extracting *increasing* amounts of surplus-value for the benefit of capitalists.

Marx charts this process historically in the *Communist Manifesto*. 'The feudal system of industry, under which industrial production was monopolized by closed guilds, now no longer sufficed for the growing wants of the new markets' (*Revolutions* 68). And he outlines it conceptually in *Capital*, volume 1. 'By turning his money into commodities which serve as the building material for a new product . . . the capitalist simultaneously transforms value . . . into capital'. Marx defines capital as 'value which can perform its own expansion, an animated monster' (*Capital* 302).

Marx's view of capitalists is one which proceeds from a high level of theoretical abstraction to the illumination and explanation of observable social phenomena within a functioning system. Hence in developing a view of capitalists he proceeds from the dynamics of the economy, rather than from the behaviour of capitalists as actual individuals. Capitalists, for Marx, are capital personified. The soul of the capitalist is the soul of capital, and capital lives only as a vampire by 'sucking living labour, and lives the more, the more labour it sucks'. Capital has one sole driving force, Marx claims, the drive to create surplus-value. Since surplus-value is but excess exchange-value, and since value is a purely quantitative measure which may numerically increase to infinity, the drive for surplus-labour is by definition a 'boundless thirst', a 'werewolf-like hunger' that respects neither human needs nor frailties (*Capital* 342, 345, 353).

Other systems of production have generated an economic surplus and have measured it as quantities of useful products. The introduction of money as a representation of exchange-value opens the way to a calculated and calculating system. In Marx's view the law of value and its corollary surplus-value are manifested in the economic movement of individual capitals and ultimately in the consciousness of individual capitalists as the motivation which drives them to eliminate competitors.

Marx's specification of the way that the 'thirst' for surplus-value operates on capitalists, who then exploit workers, takes up the major portion of *Capital*, volume 1. It makes the most impressive case for the utility of his theoretical work in social **science** and political action.

In Marx's view capitalists have an obvious interest in an unlimited extension of the working day, since with every extra increment of time beyond what is necessary to cover the workers' wages, the capitalist gains an increment of surplus-value. Marx refers to this as the production of absolute surplus-value.

But capitalists also have an interest in keeping wages as low as possible, below subsistence in individual cases, but at subsistence if the system as a whole is to continue. For the system to function a working class is continuously required to contribute the labour-power that uniquely produces new value and ultimately the profits that accrue to capitalists. Any shortening of the labour-time socially necessary for the production of a commodity is defined by Marx as an increase in the productivity of labour. Such increases ultimately reduce the amount of labour embodied in the subsistence commodities that workers use their wages to buy. Thus the cost of labour-power drops for the capitalist as the productivity of labour rises, and capital has in Marx's words 'an imminent drive, and a constant tendency, towards increasing the productivity of labour, in order to cheapen commodities and, by cheapening commodities, to cheapen the worker' (*Capital* 436–7). That process is described by Marx as an increase in relative surplus-value.

Productivity is also increased through co-operation, the creation of a new productive force as labourers combine in industrial production under capitalist direction. 'The combined working day produces a greater quantity of use-values than an equal sum of isolated working days', Marx writes, and 'the command of capital develops into a requirement for carrying on the labour process itself' (*Capital* 447, 448).

Marx charts a further development – manufacture. This arises as independent trades are combined as partial operations in the production of one particular commodity. After a certain point different trades lose their independence. Alternatively manufacture arises from the splitting up of one particular handicraft into detailed operations. At a certain point each operation becomes the exclusive function of a particular worker in one enterprise. Either way, manufacture creates 'a productive mechanism whose organs are human beings'. This insures 'a continuity, a uniformity, a regularity, an order, and even an intensity of labour' quite different from that found in independent handicrafts or simple co-operation (*Capital* 457, 465).

Marx concludes that as the productivity of labour is increased through manufacture, the requirement for raw materials and machines must grow. Thus it is a law that 'the minimum amount of capital which the capitalist must possess has to go on increasing' (*Capital* 480).

The introduction of machinery is then distinguished by Marx from manufacture, because manufacture involves revisions in the tasks done by people in combination, whereas the introduction of machinery makes the instruments of labour the focus of attention for capitalists. Thus human forces are replaced by natural ones, such as water-power, and the production process itself is analysed with a view to removing tools from human hands and fitting them into machines. Productive processes are examined and broken down into different phases, so that the natural sciences can be applied to technological problems. This has very pronounced effects on workers employed in capitalist firms. Machinery, Marx writes, 'becomes an industrial form of perpetual motion' which pushes against 'certain natural limits in the shape of weak bodies and the strong wills of its human assistants' (*Capital* 526).

Two other consequences follow. Machinery makes possible an intensification of human labour, as humans can be raced to keep up with machines. And while factory employment draws more and more people, especially women and children, into its net, the number of workers for a given amount of capital actually decreases as highly productive machines are introduced to replace less productive human beings. This occurs when the cost of machines falls below the cost of the labour-power they can replace. Marx is then able to argue that surplus-value, hence profits, will tend to fall compared with total capital invested in machines, raw materials and wages. On that basis he formulates a law of the tendency of the rate of profit to decline, though he specifies numerous countervailing factors. Capitalists are thus caught in an increasingly competitive struggle to invest in machines in order to increase the productivity of labour and thereby cheapen the commodities produced. But they are necessarily inhibited when profits diminish with respect to the cost of new investment.

Capital itself is a coercive relation, Marx argues, because in its drive to extract as much surplus-labour as possible from workers, it compels them to work longer and harder than is necessary to fulfil their own needs and those of their dependants. Though the increased productivity of labour results in cheap manufactured goods available in exchange for the money-wages of workers, and in some instances in a rising standard of living, the greater part of the benefit of the increased productivity of labour accrues to capitalists as goods and leisure. 'Division of labour within the workshop implies the undisputed authority of the capitalist', Marx writes. He concludes in political terms that 'the capitalist formulates his autocratic power over his workers like a private legislator' (*Capital* 476–7, 549–50).

Marx has in essence not so much traced politics to economics as made the workplace political by definition, arguing that out of certain social relations of production – capitalist and worker – arise the most important forces of coercion and control in society and in the state. There is thus no break between the 'economic' and the 'political' levels in society or in social science. Capitalists as individuals and as a class have a role in the factory that is just as much political as economic when they extract surplus-labour from workers by lengthening the working day, intensifying labour and increasing its productivity. Workers as individuals, and taken collectively as a class, struggle against this in a manner that is just as political as it is economic when they resist the way that their bodies, lives, health, family relations and all other aspects of well-being are sacrificed to the determining purpose of capitalist production. Capitalism is 'the greatest possible production of surplus-value, hence the greatest possible exploitation of labour-power by the capitalist' (*Capital* 449).

Marx's conceptualization of politics as proceeding from the workplace, and of economic interests as underlying the political process, are two tremendous virtues of his work, not because they are somehow correct conceptualizations for every circumstance, but because they deepen our understanding of social action. Moreover his view has a distinct political utility in that he can conceive of no ultimate justification for the control of important resources in society by some individuals or classes at the expense of others. Any such justifications partake of **ideology**.

Criticisms of Marx's theoretical work do not entirely vitiate the strengths outlined above. Profit-making is an important dynamic in industrial society, and the resulting distribution of benefits and burdens on the one hand, and political control or subjugation on the other, are arguably our most significant social problems. Marx's is the most theoretically thorough and politically radical work on capitalism that we possess.

FURTHER READING

A Marx Dictionary

alienation	**labour**
class	**mode of production**
communism	**revolution**
exploitation	**science**
fetishism of commodities	**state**
ideology	**value**

Marx's writings
Capital, especially pp. 247–80, 643–54, 762–72, 794–802
Revolutions, 'Communist Manifesto', pp. 67–87

Secondary sources
Brewer (1984), especially chapters 1–8
Carver (1982), especially chapter 6
Cleaver (1979), especially parts II–V
Fine (1975), especially chapters 2–8
Giddens (1985), especially chapters 5–6
Suchting (1983), especially part III
Wallerstein (1983), especially chapters 1–2
Walton and Gamble (1972), especially chapter 7

class

A crucial term in Marx's political and theoretical work, but one he fails to define explicitly. Class, for Marx, is the most obvious manifestation of the truth of his famous proposition that the 'social existence' of people 'determines their consciousness'. Yet in the most succinct summary of his theory that he left us, the 1859 'Preface' to *A Contribution to the Critique of Political Economy*, the term 'class' is curiously absent (*Early Writing* 424–8).

Perhaps this is for political reasons. In his critique of political economy Marx does not intend preaching **communism** to the already converted, and he may have excluded the term as too controversial. Yet the architecture of his theory is made clear when he refers in the 'Preface' to an 'antagonism' that is not simply that of individual against individual, but 'an antagonism that emanates from the individuals' social conditions of existence'. While this is not exactly a definition of class, it helps us to identify the phenomenon as he sees it and to locate it with respect to his work on **base and superstructure** and **mode of production** (*Early Writings* 425–6).

Marx's work on contemporary **capitalism** contains his most extensive and most plausible discussion of class. In modern bourgeois society he points to new classes, new conditions of oppression, new forms of struggle. He does this in his *Economic and Philosophical Manuscripts* of 1844, where he turns most of his attention to the **alienation** of workers or proletarians. In the *Communist Manifesto* of 1848 he considers the capitalist class or bourgeoisie in the first instance and at greater length. And in *Capital*, volume 1, of 1867, he outlines the economic concepts and practices of capitalism that permit the **exploitation** of **labour** by capital and so create the two hostile classes, bourgeoisie and proletariat.

For Marx it is the development and growth of capital through the agency of capitalists or the bourgeoisie that has created the

social conditions of existence for the modern working class or
proletariat. It is the continued reproduction of those social
conditions of existence that maintains the contrasting circumstances of those who labour and those who benefit from its
exploitation. The most succinct characterization of the two
classes appears in the *Communist Manifesto*.

In the *Communist Manifesto* Marx takes a polemical approach.
This is an overtly political document reconciling the differing
views of self-proclaimed communists and promulgating the
results to the public. The work presumes the importance of the
classes 'bourgeois and proletarians' in modern society and
announces in the most sweeping terms that the 'history of all
hitherto existing society is the history of class struggles'
(*Revolutions* 67).

While the modern bourgeoisie is said to be the product of a
long course of development, the process is outlined and
simplified to the transformation of runaway serfs into chartered
burghers in the European towns of the early Middle Ages. With
the growth of world-wide markets as European navigation and
commerce improved there came the dissolution of handicraft
guilds and the development of chartered burghers into a
manufacturing middle class presiding over workshops. The final
phase of development for Marx is the establishment of modern
industry, in which steam and machinery revolutionized industrial production. The middle class of manufacturers is then
supplanted by 'industrial millionaires, the leaders of whole
industrial armies, the modern bourgeois' (*Revolutions* 67–9).

In *Capital*, volume 1, Marx reproduces this outline scheme in
the chapters on 'Co-operation', 'Division of Labour and Manufacture', and 'Machinery and Large-scale Industry', albeit
within the analytical terms that define capitalist production in
his later work – **value**, money, capital, surplus-value and profit.
'The struggle between the capitalist and the wage-labourer', he
writes, 'starts with the existence of the capital-relation itself'.
The historical development of the bourgeoisie and proletariat, or
capitalists and workers, appears in the concluding section 'So-
called Primitive Accumulation'. This discussion represents a
version of the account given in the *Communist Manifesto*, though it
benefits from additional research and more time spent on
composition. 'So-called primitive accumulation', he writes, 'is

nothing else than the historical process of divorcing the producer from the means of production'. And, he adds, 'the methods of primitive accumulation are anything but idyllic' (*Capital* 553, 874–5).

Marx portrays the bourgeoisie in the *Communist Manifesto* in a way that distinguishes it from earlier industrial classes which aimed to conserve unaltered the modes of production from which they derived their social position. By contrast the bourgeoisie 'cannot exist without constantly revolutionizing the instruments of production'. During a mere one hundred years the bourgeoisie has created 'more massive and more colossal productive forces than have all preceding generations together' (*Revolutions* 70, 72).

In the *Communist Manifesto* it is 'naked self-interest' that drives the process of capital accumulation. In *Capital*, volume 1, accumulation is presented as the drive to self-expansion inherent in capital. Either way Marx pictures the bourgeoisie pursuing a limitless quest for profit that distributes the class over the 'whole surface of the globe' where it supplants 'old-established national industries'. New industries, 'whose introduction becomes a life and death question for all civilized nations', are then required. This process leaves remaining between persons no other nexus than callous 'cash payment' (*Revolution* 70–1).

Marx presents the bourgeoisie as ruthless cosmopolitan egoists who reduce all values – he mentions personal worth, the honour due to the professions, religious fervour, chivalry, chartered freedoms and family life – to mere money relations. Some of those social relationships, he suggests, may have been exploitation 'veiled by religious and political illusions' as detailed in his work on **ideology** and the **fetishism of commodities**. For veiled exploitation the bourgeoisie substitutes the 'naked, shameless, direct, brutal exploitation' that he portrays in *Capital*, volume 1. The limitless drive for profit pushes capitalists to increase the exploitation of the work-force, whether the capitalists personally want to do this or not (*Revolutions* 70–2).

For Marx the fundamental conditions of capitalist exploitation are present when there is 'the confrontation of, and the contact between, two very different kinds of commodity owners'. This creates two classes in society.

Firstly, there are the owners of productive resources, such as machines and raw materials, who want to expand the amount of value at their disposal by buying the labour-power of others and thus appropriating the product. This is the sole way that new value can be created, according to Marx.

And secondly there is the class of labourers, sellers of their own labour-power, which the bourgeoisie has in effect called into existence. These are 'free workers' who are not wholly owned as a productive resource (as slaves would be) nor are they owners of productive resources other than labour-power (like land-owning peasants). Free workers are also different from serfs. While serfs may control certain productive resources and some of their own labour-time, other productive resources are controlled by their superiors, who can claim some of their labour-time without payment.

Thus the process of creating capital divorces workers from the ownership of any of the conditions of their labour. Free workers, as sought by the bourgeoisie, have 'nothing to sell except their own skins' (*Capital* 873–4). In the *Communist Manifesto* he describes the proletariat as 'a class of labourers, who live only so long as they find work, and who find work only so long as their labour increases capital' (*Revolutions* 73). They are a commodity and consequently exposed to competition and market fluctu-ations. Some of those market forces are movingly described in the *Economic and Philosophical Manuscripts* (*Early Writings* 282–9), and in the chapters on 'The Working Day' and the section on 'Wages' in *Capital*, volume 1 (*Capital* 340–416, 675–706).

Competition in the market affects bourgeois and proletarian alike, Marx comments in the *Communist Manifesto*, whether the market is in goods or labour. The lower strata of the middle class, which cannot compete on price with the industrial enterprises controlled by capitalists, sink gradually into the proletariat, where they have to compete as sellers of labour, a competition from which captialists derive the major benefit as it keeps wages low (*Revolutions* 75–6).

The crucial point in Marx's political theory is precisely his belief that competition between individual workers to undercut each other on wages must give way, ultimately, to the 'organization of the proletarians into a class'. Individual workers, rather than competing with each other, must form combinations or trade unions and thus co-operate as a group to keep wages up and pursue a common struggle against the interests of capitalists. 'Here and there', Marx notes in the *Communist Manifesto*, 'the contest breaks out into riots.' 'Every class struggle', he generalizes, 'is a political struggle' (*Revolutions* 76).

Such political action, in Marx's time, was a matter of compelling the **state** to recognize the interests of workers by limiting the working day and securing health and safety inspections. He comments somewhat cryptically in the *Communist Manifesto* that these political gains were achieved 'by taking advantage of the divisions among the bourgeoisie itself', an allusion perhaps to conflicts between the differing interests of industrial, financial and land-owning capitalists that could be exploited politically (*Revolutions* 76).

Indeed Marx suggests that the industrial bourgeoisie may call on the proletariat as an ally in political struggles against financial interests or a foreign bourgeoisie, thus schooling the proletariat in practical politics. Even bourgeois ideologists, 'who have raised themselves to the level of comprehending theoretically the historical movement as a whole', may come over to the proletariat and help pursue a proletarian **revolution** (*Revolutions* 76–7).

For Marx the dynamic of capitalism is such that the class structure of society will simplify into two distinct interests as class struggle sharpens up. The proletarian cause is 'the interest of the immense majority' that will supplant an obviously unworkable minority interest in production for profit, and he predicts that pauperism will develop more rapidly than population and wealth. It becomes evident, he prognosticates, that the bourgeoisie is unfit to rule because it is incompetent. It cannot help letting workers sink into such a state that the bourgeoisie must feed the proletariat, instead of the reverse (*Revolutions* 78–9).

Class relations play a further part in the overall struggle, however, as the lower middle class, small manufacturer, shopkeeper, artisan and peasant may fight against the bourgeoisie in defence of their present interests, but not as a rule in aid of their future interests as proletarians. By struggling against the march of capitalism, they are not merely conservative, Marx opines, but reactionary. They make unreliable allies in pro-

letarian politics, as does the 'dangerous class' of lumpen-
proletarians or ruffians who can be bribed to support the
bourgeoisie (*Revolutions* 77).

Using the materials of the *Communist Manifesto* Marx pursues a
class politics that combines partisan commitment and intellectual sophistication in equal measure. It is commitment, however, that reconciles his polemical generalizations about class
struggle and political action with the varied descriptive categories and subtleties that also figure in the *Communist Manifesto*
and illuminate his accounts of contemporary politics, especially
in France.

Marx assesses the course of revolutionary and counter-
revolutionary events in France for an international audience in
three works, *The Class Struggles in France* of 1850, *The Eighteenth
Brumaire of Louis Bonaparte* of 1852 and *The Civil War in France* of
1871. In his political reflections on contemporary history he uses
a vast array of categories referring to classes and class fractions,
such as financial aristocracy, industrial bourgeoisie, peasant
class, proletariat, lumpenproletariat and great land-owners. The
cast of characters in the political dramas includes party
politicians, political parties and coteries, the army and national
guard, ideological representatives and spokesmen, secret societies and public clubs. The economic interests of individual
classes and other groups are detailed by Marx, but these are
sometimes compromised, misunderstood or defied in actual
practice, as we learn from his narrative. For instance tradition,
rather than economic interest, is specifically mentioned as a
major determinant of behaviour when he comments that the
'tradition of the dead generations weighs like a nightmare on the
minds of the living' (*Surveys* 146).

Marx uses his aphorism that every class struggle is a political
struggle to relate political struggles to social classes and to
portray social classes as political agents. In relating political
struggles to social classes, his approach is not reductionist,
because not all political activity is traced to economic interest.
And his portrayal of social classes as political agents is not
exclusionary, since other political actors, individual and collective, are admitted.

Class struggle, in Marx's work, is compatible not only with
overt fighting and opposition, but also with veiled hostility. Even

more strikingly he considers class struggle to be compatible with individual and collective unconsciousness and illusion about the very elements of economic conflict that he is convinced are at work in society. For Marx class interests may diverge, converge or compromise depending on events and the way that individuals assess them.

Marx's 'class struggle' is more like a hypothesis about what politics might be than a proposition about what it must be by definition. This view makes his prediction that the class character of society is simplifying logically compatible with his analysis of contemporary events where he uses a very large number of class categories, class fractions and non-class political actors. By publicizing his analysis of contemporary events he intended to push political reality towards his generalizations and predictions.

Marx's concept of class is aphoristic, since class struggle is captured 'in a word' within the concepts oppressor and oppressed, as he put it in the *Communist Manifesto*. And it is stipulative in that examples – 'freeman and slave, patrician and plebeian, lord and serf, guildmaster and journeyman' – are supposed to do for definitions (*Revolutions* 68). But his view that history is the history of class struggles has been profoundly influential in political analysis and action.

FURTHER READING

A Marx Dictionary

alienation	ideology
base and superstructure	labour
capitalism	mode of production
communism	revolution
exploitation	state
fetishism of commodities	value

Marx's writings.
First International, 'Civil War in France', especially pp. 206–10
Revolutions, 'Communist Manifesto', especially pp. 67–87

Surveys, 'Class Struggles in France', especially pp. 35–40; 'Eighteenth Brumaire', especially pp. 156–69, 234–49

Secondary sources

Avineri (1970), especially chapters 2–3
Carver (1982), especially chapter 4
Giddens (1981), especially chapters 5, 7, 9
Roemer (1982), especially chapters 2, 4
Suchting (1983), especially chapter 11
Walton and Gamble (1972), especially chapter 7
Wood (1981), especially chapter VI and part 4

communism

The term Marx uses to describe a society of the future in which **class** conflict will be abolished. It is also the name of the political movement with which he identifies himself.

In communist society the industrial technology associated with **capitalism**, the modern bourgeois **mode of production**, will be retained and developed. New relations of production will be established in correspondence with this economic **base, and** a new **superstructure** of social relationships will ensure that the interests of the whole community of producers will be paramount, rather than the interest one class has in the **exploitation** of another.

Because of the predictable resistance of property-owning classes to the communist **revolution** that Marx envisages, the struggle to reorganize society in the interests of the proletariat or working class will almost certainly be violent. Ultimately for Marx communism entails the abolition of familar features of capitalist society – private ownership of the means of production, the use of of **labour** to produce goods with a **value** in exchange, the **fetishism of commodities** which arises from that particular way of organizing the economy, the **state** as an agency of class oppression and **alienation** in all its aspects.

For Marx the contemporary communist movement is supposed to be the bridge between the political and theoretical advocates of communism and the exploited proletarians who are to build it. But he argues that at the outset the proletarian movement should help the bourgeoisie by fighting any feudal or other reactionary powers in order to establish regimes favourable to bourgeois participation in the economy and politics. This entails a temporary alliance between proletarians and their ultimate enemies. Putting this across to the working class and its representatives creates an extremely complex political agenda, since communists are to serve the interests of the bourgeoisie and simultaneously oppose their exploitation of proletarians.

The communist movement for Marx is in essence international, owing to the world-wide penetration by capitalist
industry of non-capitalist societies. But in fact the fight for
proletarian interests is to be conducted in the first instance
within nation-states. Thus any local section of the very decen-
tralized communist movement which Marx supports faces a
daunting array of potential conflicts of interest within the
working class itself.

Marx boldly allies the communist movement, as he conceives
it, with all the interests of the proletariat, who as industrial
workers were admittedly a minority even in the most developed
countries of the 1840s. But according to his view of the
inherently expansionist character of capitalist production, this
proletarian class will become a majority as the structure of
bourgeois society increasingly corresponds to 'two great camps',
bourgeoisie and proletariat, as he put it in the *Communist
Manifesto* of 1848 (*Revolutions* 68).

Marx claims to eschew 'sectarian principles' and mere 'ideas'
invented or discovered by 'this or that would-be universal
reformer'. Instead the theoretical conclusions of communists are
to express 'actual relations springing from an existing class
struggle'. 'Communists fight for the attainment of the immediate
aims, for the enforcement of the momentary interests of the
working class', Marx states, 'but in the movement of the present,
they also represent and take care of the future of that movement'
(*Revolutions* 79–80, 97).

There is a certain advantage of immediacy in this approach to
politics, provided that the organizing principles used to interpret
actual social relations and the existing class struggle can be
related plausibly to current concerns and are explicit enough in
themselves to inspire confidence. Despite Marx's view that
communism is already a self-conscious social movement, he is
necessarily compelled to speculate on the features of a communist society, since otherwise there would be no way for him to
encourage what he considered communist within the contemporary working-class movement and to discourage de-
partures from this standard. His political method is thus
precariously balanced between the exposition of workers' views
and the promulgation of a personal vision. Provided the vision is

presented in sufficiently general terms his claim that it coincides
with current political thinking in the communist movement can
be maintained. However, this generality makes it difficult to
specify the terms of his ideal society with much precision.

Marx's most abstract and visionary account of non-alienated
social relations occurs in an early manuscript of 1844, the
Excerpts from James Mill's 'Elements of Political Economy'. In a few
lines he sketches a view of the relations between individuals and
the products of their labour, and between individuals themselves, in which labour will cease to be an unpleasant activity
that they seek to minimize, and will become instead 'the free
expression and hence the enjoyment of life' (*Early Writings* 277–
8).

The *Communist Manifesto*, somewhat more generally, refers to a
society in which 'the free development of each is the condition for
the free development of all.' This would come about through the
introduction of a 'communistic mode of producing and appropriating material products' that entails the abolition of private
property. This abolition, in Marx's view, 'deprives no one of the
power to appropriate the products of society', only 'the power to
subjugate the labour of others by means of such appropriation'
(*Revolutions* 80, 82, 87).

In *Capital*, volume 1, Marx contrasts capitalist society with a
hypothetical association of free workers who hold the means of
production in common and who regard their total product as a
social product. Part of this product replenishes the production
process and therefore remains social, and part is consumed by
members of the association as their means of subsistence.

The problem of dividing a social product amongst consumers
marks a boundary line between a transitional phase of society
sometimes referred to as socialism, and a higher phase associated with communism as it might be fully developed. In *Capital*,
volume 1, Marx comments that the principles according to
which the social product is divided may be expected to vary with
the different ways that production is organized and 'the corresponding level of social development of the producers' (*Capital*
171–2).

In his *Critique of the Gotha Programme* of 1875 Marx expands on
the way that such a transitional phase might be organized. The
labour expended on products would no longer appear as their

monetary value. Instead in an early phase of communist society, stamped in every respect 'with the birthmarks of the old capitalist society from whose womb it has emerged', the individual producer would get back from society what has been contributed, a quantity of labour, after a deduction for social purposes. Thus labour certificates might be awarded to workers, and goods costing an equivalent amount of labour could be obtained in exchange (*First International* 345–6).

This phase is merely transitional, because using labour as a standard measure rewards workers with goods according to their physical or intellectual skills, fortitude or efficiency. While this inequality does not produce class divisions, 'because everyone is just a worker like everyone else', Marx does not consider this socialist phase fully adequate. In a more advanced communist society, when individuals are no longer enslaved within the division of labour, when 'the antithesis between intellectual and physical labour has disappeared', when labour itself has become a 'vital need', when productive power has increased and 'the springs of cooperative wealth flow more abundantly', then communism will prevail, because each will contribute according to ability and receive according to need (*First International* 345–7). Freely associated producers, Marx comments in *Capital*, volume 1, will in that circumstance have brought the process of material production under their conscious and planned control (*Capital* 173).

In this highest phase of communism Marx assumes away a large number of economic problems so familiar to us as features of production and distribution themselves that his view seems entirely unsubstantiated. These are the problems associated with producer-incentives, rationing of goods amongst consumers, establishing overall levels of production, agreeing criteria for distribution and fixing the terms of international trade. Whether he envisages a mechanized process producing so many goods so abundantly that efficiency in production and rationing in distribution will cease to be issues, or whether he foresees economizing on resources and agreeing on distribution as problems to be ironed out in the social process of planning, is not at all clear. For Marx communism is industrial production built anew on principles just the opposite of those required by capitalism, the object of his most extensive intellectual inquiries.

FURTHER READING

A Marx Dictionary

alienation

base and superstructure

capitalism

class

exploitation

fetishism of commodities

labour

mode of production

revolution

state

value

Marx's writings

Capital, especially pp. 171–3

Early Writings, 'Excerpts from James Mill', especially pp. 277–8

First International, 'Critique of the Gotha Programme', especially pp. 343–8

Revolutions, 'Communist Manifesto', especially pp. 79–87

Secondary sources

Avineri (1970), especially chapter 8

Carver (1982), especially chapter 5

Maguire (1972), especially chapters 4, 7

Maguire (1978), especially chapter 8

Nove (1985), especially part 1

Suchting (1983), especially chapters 2–4, 19, 21

dialectic

A term that figures importantly in the philosophy of G. W. F. Hegel, who took it from the tradition of classical Greek philosophy and altered its definition very considerably. In the classical tradition 'dialectic' referred to a kind of discussion in which arguments were posed and refuted in succession. Grasping the conclusion in full depended on absorbing the successive positive claims and their negations.

Marx conceives of dialectic as a tool in pursuing his **science** of society. He looks for 'contradictions', such as oppositions of economic interest in society, and argues that political conflicts are best understood in relation to them.

In his critical writing Marx seeks to discredit the work of certain followers of Hegel as intellectually untenable and politically damaging to the cause of **communism**. To do this he needs to link them with what he believes to be spurious in Hegel's work, especially his conception of the dialectic.

Marx objects to Hegel's philosophy for its idealist assumptions, that is, the view that reality is ultimately conceptual and is to be accounted for in no other terms. Marx counters with a **materialism**, sometimes referred to as 'true' or 'new', which presupposes the material reality of the world including the material aspects of human beings. Their will and consciousness, whether ultimately material or not, are necessarily engaged in the productive activities required to sustain the species, as well as in other intellectual and artistic pursuits. This philosophical presumption is closer to what is nowadays known as realism, as opposed to materialisms which assume that all phenomena are ultimately material, rather than ideal or supernatural.

In his *Economic and Philosophical Manuscripts* of 1844 Marx refers to Hegel's concept as a 'dialectic of negativity as the moving and producing principle', but one which in Hegel's idealist philosophy always presents the actual progress of history as a development of concepts. This amounts, in Marx's view, to an **ideology**, in that real events and interests are made mysterious by their subsumption into a highly abstract rationalization of human experience (*Early Writings* 385–6). Thus in an 'Afterword' (1873) to *Capital*, volume 1, of 1867, Marx comments that his 'dialectical method is, in its foundations, not only different from the Hegelian, but exactly opposite to it'. Hegel has transformed the process of thinking into an independent subject which appears in a mysterious way to be the creator of the real world, whereas for Marx the real world is human society in which human subjects have thoughts. Ideas are the result of actual minds reflecting on the material world within which human society functions (*Capital* 102–3).

Hegel's presentation of human experience as a dialectic of philosophical concepts derives its developmental qualities from a kind of negativity. As one concept confronts another in a definition or statement, so an apparently positive relation is succeeded in Hegel's mind by one of contradiction.

Contradiction, for Hegel, is not held in abhorrence as a relation to be avoided, as other logicians often stipulate. Rather he envisages contradiction as a dynamic feature of conceptual relations such that new conceptions arise which supersede and contain the contradiction, yet do not formally abolish it. Understanding thus ascends to a higher level, a negation of the negation, or supersession to which the initial contradiction had contributed positively.

Hegel explains that his conception of the dialectic grasps the positive aspects of an apparently negative relationship, that of conceptual contradiction. For example, he claims that the concept 'identity' contains its own contradiction, the concept 'difference', and that the concept 'opposite' arises from this contradiction, negating and unifying it at the same time. He regards this process of transcending contradictions as the essential movement driving his philosophical system towards absolute knowledge.

Marx's comments on the dialectic took place in a highly political context. Initially he criticized its use by Hegelians whose works and political views were current in the 1840s. But Hegelian philosophy and politics had altogether declined by the 1860s when Marx was publishing his critical analysis of

capitalism. At that point he was concerned to emphasize that he formulated his own concept of the dialectic, albeit through a transformation of Hegel's, because he wished to distinguish himself from the British school of political economy. Since a good deal of Marx's account of capitalism was based on amendments to Adam Smith and David Ricardo on their own economic terms, it was easy for some reviewers cited by Marx to dismiss his work as merely derivative and to miss its politically subversive character. Other critics grasped that the presentation of economic material in *Capital*, volume 1, was dialectical in a manner related to the idealist tradition in German philosophy, but dismissed this as Hegelian sophistry and rejected the book altogether or suggested that its economic content ought to be evaluated separately from the confusing way in which it was presented.

Thus Marx had to show his readers exactly what he had taken from Hegel, what he had rejected, and why a concept of dialectic was necessary at all in order to present a critical account of capitalist society that was built on the firm foundations of the economic science that Smith and Ricardo had initiated. His explanation of the dialectic was put forward in this complicated intellectual context because, in his view, the political thrust of his work would be vitiated if ill-informed and partisan critics were allowed to present his masterpiece in a misleading way.

The dialectic, in rational form, so Marx argues, is 'a scandal and an abomination to the bourgeoisie, and its doctrinaire spokesmen'. This is because dialectical analysis includes in any 'positive understanding of what exists a simultaneous recognition of its negation, its inevitable destruction'. Moreover it also presupposes that every historically developed form of society has a transient aspect, in that its elements are in a fluid state, in motion. The thrust of a dialectical analysis is towards the exposure of the contradictions in any socio-economic system from which the **class** struggle arises. In its very essence, he writes, the dialectic is 'critical and revolutionary' (*Capital* 98–103).

Engels interpreted the dialectic rather differently, but attributed his own interpretation to Marx. In Engels's view the dialectic was the essential feature of a scientific method, universal in scope and first formulated by Marx. It was based on a crudely materialist inversion of Hegel's idealism, a view that contradictions are inherent in all reality, and a conviction that universal laws, of which he formulated three, represent valid results derived from applying the dialectical method to nature, history and logic. The unitary methodology and the encyclopaedic pretensions of such a grandiose system of interpretation were never explicitly endorsed by Marx. Whether or not they are reflected in his work is a matter of controversy.

Neither Marx, nor Engels, nor Hegel endorses a concept of dialectic as a sequence of thesis–antithesis–synthesis. Nothing in their works justifies such a simplification, and it contradicts the various interpretations of the term offered by all three. Indeed Marx criticized it as naïve.

FURTHER READING

A Marx Dictionary

capitalism	**ideology**
class	**materialism**
communism	**science**

Marx's writings
Capital, especially pp. 94–103, 729, 744n
Early Writings, 'Economic and Philosophical Manuscripts', especially pp. 379–400

Secondary sources
Callinicos (1983), especially chapters 2–3
Carver (1982), especially chapter 4
Mepham (1979a), especially chapters 1–3
Norman (1980), especially chapters 1–2
Sayer (1979), especially chapter 6
Suchting (1983), especially chapter 18
Walton and Gamble (1972), especially chapter 3
Wood (1981), especially part 5

exploitation

A term Marx uses in referring to the production and distribution of goods in societies where the **mode of production** provides a surplus over subsistence requirements. His theory of exploitation is most elaborately developed in *Capital*, volume 1, of 1867, for the analysis of **capitalism**. But the concept itself is historically more general for him and is a reworking in more specific terms of certain aspects of **alienation**. 'Wherever a part of society possesses the monopoly of the means of production', he writes, 'the worker, free or unfree, must add to the labour-time necessary for his own maintenance an extra quantity of labour-time in order to produce the means of subsistence for the owner of the means of production.' Such owners could be, for example, Athenian or Roman aristocrats, Norman barons, American slave-owners, modern landlords or capitalists (*Capital* 344–5). In short, exploiters are those who acquire the benefits of production, in cash or kind, by virtue of their control over tools, machines, land or raw materials necessary to production.

To develop his concept of exploitation Marx presents us with workers who produce goods, some of which are distributed to owners or superiors who control the means of production. Though workers in society characteristically produce goods for distribution to those who are too young, too old or otherwise unsuited for work, it is the production of goods which accrue to individuals by virtue of their ownership rights or social superiority that draws Marx's attention. Those without such ownership or customary rights to resources are typically workers, in Marx's view, even if they are at times unemployed or otherwise excluded from the productive process altogether by those who control access to the land, tools, or raw materials that are required for any production to take place. Those not suited for work are by definition dependants in some sense, rather than workers, though they may coincidentally be owners or proprietors of productive resources.

The access to goods or to income enjoyed by owners of productive resources is not derived from any inability to function as workers. A theory that explained ownership rights in the means of production that proceeds analytically from the material needs of children, the elderly and the disabled would have amused Marx intensely, since justifications for ownership rights in productive resources characteristically proceed from arguments about entrepreneurs.

However, Marx's own theory depends on certain stipulations concerning workers, owners and **labour** itself.

1 Only workers contribute the labour that transforms raw materials into goods. Ownership or control of the instruments of production, natural resources or the means to purchase them does not constitute work (*Capital* 283–91).

2 Where a surplus product arises, it is considered by Marx to be the result of surplus labour, not the result of some natural or accidental process (*Capital* 129–31).

3 If some of what is produced is distributed to certain persons because they own productive resources, there is exploitation. There may be many other reasons for differential distribution of goods and differential liability to work. Whether such differences and the reasons for them are justified or not is an issue quite separate from exploitation (*Capital* 291–2).

Thus for Marx exploitation applies to economies where the means of production are controlled by a part of society, because this allows those who control productive resources to take advantage of those who do not. The basic criterion underlying this theory of exploitation is a distinction between work and ownership rather than the more complicated premises necessary to make goods or labour-products commensurable with labour itself. He additionally accepts such a view, but at its most basic level his theory of exploitation does not depend on it, since owners of the means of production need only get the benefit of products produced by workers for the charge of exploitation to stick.

Difficulties arise for Marx's theory when there are owners of the means of production who also work, whether in their own businesses or elsewhere, and workers who also own the means of production, whether for their own activities or someone else's. Thus his overall categories of exploited worker and exploiter as owner of the means of production do not translate easily to the level of real individuals in society, who may participate in both. Nor do the categories exploiter and exploited generate an unambiguous **class** struggle, because there may be relatively few clear-cut examples of either. This poses problems for Marx's social **science**, as well as for his politics. His concept of exploitation is supposed to have validity as a characterization of the way that work and ownership of the means of production interact in certain societies, even when the terms exploiter and exploited cannot be employed with respect to individual circumstances.

Marx argued that under capitalism exploitation can be measured with some precision. In the capitalist production of goods and services as commodities with a **value**, the values that all such goods have on the market represents the amount of labour-time socially necessary on average to produce them at any given moment. When this value is realized as goods exchange for money, which itself represents the labour-time required on average to produce the precious metals which back up currency and credit, some of the value returns to workers as wages and some accrues to the owners of productive resources as rent and profits.

Thus the typical working day can be divided into two portions. Marx calls the first portion necessary labour-time, since goods produced in that period represent the value which will pay the workers' wages. And he calls the second surplus labour-time, since goods produced in that period represent value which accrues to capitalists as a surplus over the wages they pay out. The ratio of necessary to surplus labour-time defines the rate of surplus-value, 'an exact expression for the degree of exploitation of labour-power by capital, or of the worker by the capitalist' (*Capital* 326–7, 340–1).

This analysis enables Marx to argue that the rate of profit, the ratio of profits to total capital invested, is not a measure of the exploitation of labour. This is because the surplus-value from which profits are solely derived is wholly a product of the new value created uniquely by workers in the labour process. It is not attributable to any values represented in productive resources. Those values are merely transferred to goods as materials are used up in production. A rate of profit of 10 per cent, so Marx, argues, might therefore disguise a rate of exploitation of 100 per cent for example, because profits are large compared with wages but small compared with the value represented by machinery and raw materials in an enterprise.

Capitalists are exploiters, on Marx's definition, and workers are exploited, since the rights of each class to the values realized on the market are diametrically opposed. In Marx's view workers produce goods with values-in-exchange which are wholly controlled by owners of the means of production. It is obviously in their interests to minimize the return of any value at all to workers and to maximize returns to themselves, which Marx terms surplus-value.

Marx argues that the capitalist system tends towards subsistence wages for workers, since the labour force will generally have to be reproduced from generation to generation, though in some circumstances owners of capital may well pay wages below the subsistence requirements of workers and their dependants. Alternatively the system allows the payment of wages well in excess of subsistence, whilst still permitting capitalists a considerable surplus for their own disposal as investment or consumption, without thereby abolishing exploitation. So long as access to the means of production and to the benefits of the productive process is controlled by virtue of ownership rights, exploitation as Marx defines it will persist as a structural feature of society.

'The capitalist mode of production,' Marx comments in the *Critique of the Gotha Programme* of 1875, rests on the fact that the material conditions of production are in the hands of non-workers in the form of property in capital and land, while the masses are only owners of the personal condition of production, labour power. But he envisages alternative arrangements. 'If the material conditions of production were the cooperative property of the workers themselves', he writes, 'a different distribution of the means of consumption from that of today would follow of its own accord' (*First International* 348). In his brief sketches of socialism and **communism** he suggests that exploitation will be abolished because its basic condition – ownership of the means of production by a part of society – will have been replaced through a social **revolution** instituting co-operative control of productive resources by the workers themselves.

FURTHER READING

A Marx Dictionary

alienation

capitalism

class

communism

labour

mode of production

revolution

science

value

Marx's writings

Capital, especially pp. 171–2, 344–8, 449–51, 477, 680–1, 768–70

First International, 'Critique of the Gotha Programme', especially pp. 341–8

Secondary sources

Carver (1982), especially chapter 6

Fine (1975), especially chapter 4

Hodgson (1982), especially chapter 18

Roemer (1982), especially introduction

Weeks (1981), especially chapter III

Wood (1981), especially chapter XV

fetishism of commodities

Marx uses the term 'fetishism' in a sense that predates the meaning it has acquired in modern psychological studies. For him a fetish is an inanimate object worshipped on account of its alleged inherent magical powers, an object supposedly animated by a spirit or god. Fetishism is thus the practice of worshipping such an idol.

The term 'commodity' is defined by Marx in *Capital*, volume 1, of 1867. A commodity is an external object which, through its properties, satisfies some human need or other. For Marx the commodity is a social form superimposed on material wealth which only arises in certain societies, namely those in which market relations make their appearance. Market relations presuppose the production of useful objects for exchange, and in exchange, they have a **value**.

The utility of a commodity Marx terms its use-value, which is inherent in the physical properties or qualities of the object. Use-values are the material content of wealth in any form of society whatsoever, though exactly which properties of which objects are valued at any particular time for any particular utility may vary.

While Marx presupposes that an object produced for exchange must have some use-value, his concept of value-in-exchange is not a quantification of it. There is no common measure of utility, he says, which will allow use-values of different kinds to be compared quantitatively and exchanged in equal amounts. In his view the utility of precious metals in a market economy is in their use-value as coin or bullion, a money-commodity, and this use-value is not commensurable with the utility of any particular object for which a quantity of precious metal is exchanged.

Marx notes that the exchange-value of commodities seems to be a constantly changing relation of monetary worth between useful objects, but he argues that this is mere appearance. For Marx monetary worth does not itself define exchange-value, rather monetary worth represents exchange-value when commodities other than money are set equal to a money-commodity, such as a quantity of precious metal, in the course of market exchange.

Marx rejects the view that the exchange-value of any particular commodity is unpredictably variable according to the different needs felt by consumers at different times and the supposedly very different amounts of goods or the money-commodity that they might part with in order to make the purchase. Rather he presumes that there is a certain stability in the ratios in which different commodities exchange on the market, that these stable ratios are a quantitative reflection of some element that all commodities have in common and that shifts in these ratios reflect changes in the amount of this element contained in one or both commodities equated in any typical exchange.

That common element could not be any physical or natural property of commodities, Marx argues, because it is those very properties which constitute their useful qualities or use-values. These are quantitatively measurable only as aggregates of identical objects. Exchange on the market presupposes the indiscriminate interchangeability of objects of different kinds. In Marx's view market exchange proceeds in complete abstraction from the particular physical properties or use-values of particular commodities. Therefore some common, but non-physical property must account for exchange-value, by which an exclusively quantitative relationship between different kinds of objects becomes possible. According to Marx, there is only one such property common to useful objects that are exchanged on the market. That property is being products of **labour**.

However, Marx argues that this must be labour in its abstract, quantitatively equalizable form, rather than the qualitatively different and quantitatively incommensurable forms that are manifested in real activities, e.g. carpentry, spinning etc. This abstract labour is thus a non-physical substance, since it is supposed to consist in identical units derived from the total labour-power of society taken as one homogeneous mass. The exchange-value of a commodity, he concludes, represents the amount of abstract labour that is necessary on average to produce an average example under normal conditions in a society using an average degree of skill and intensity (*Capital* 125–31).

Marx concludes that our use of the concept 'commodity' to refer to useful objects exchanged on the market is not the obvious, trivial matter that it appears at first sight. Rather, a close analysis reveals a mystical or enigmatic character in the concept that is overlooked in the commonplace **ideology** of capitalist society. In Marx's view the products of human hands appear in society as autonomous entities with a life of their own which enter into relations with each other and with human beings. In that striking way he characterizes the market relationships of commodities to each other in the real world as analogous to a 'misty realm' of religion, a fantasy world in which imaginary entities exercise their wills on each other and impose them on subservient human beings.

Commodity fetishism arises through a process of substitution. The abstract equality between different kinds of human labour appears in society as their equality as values-in-exchange. The measurement of human labour by the time during which it is expended appears in society as the amount of value inherent in commodities. And the productive relationship between workers themselves appears in society as the relations of market exchange, since workers are only organized for production as and when the market permits.

Workers rightly perceive that they do not experience direct social relations between persons at work. Instead they experience 'material relations of persons', or 'reification of persons', since they compete to sell their labour-power as a commodity. They also experience 'social relations between things', or 'personification of things', since it is the exchange-relations of their products that count for more in social life than the real relations of persons.

Market relations between commodities are not merely a harmless substitutional form for the labour, amount of labour and employment of labour that actually occur in production. As exchange-relations proceed there arises a 'movement of things' which is far from being under the control of the workers who make them. In fact this movement controls the workers themselves. An example is the shift of workers from one branch of production to another or into unemployment as a result of market forces (*Capital* 163–8, 209).

For Marx the fetishism of commodities is the specific type of **alienation** that arises in the modern bourgeois **mode of production** (*Capital* 719, 799). In his exposition he specifies the mechanism by which alienation originates in commodity-producing and capitalist societies, and in his social **science** it unifies **exploitation**, unemployment and economic crises into a comprehensive theory.

Commodity fetishism is not present, by definition, in societies where market relations, the production of goods for exchange, have not yet developed. The practice originates only when a useful object is superfluous to the immediate needs of its owner and there exists a tacit agreement amongst people to treat each other as independent persons, the private owners of alienable things. This relationship of isolation and foreignness or alienation does not exist, Marx claims, for members of primitive communities such as patriarchal families, communes in India or the Inca state. He argues that the exchange of commodities begins at the boundaries of such communities where they come into contact with members of other groups. Thus commodities develop in the external relations of communities, and the production of surplus goods for exchange then occurs by reaction within the community itself.

The 'quantitative exchange-relation is at first determined purely by chance', Marx writes. As the need for useful objects produced by others is gradually established in a community, so constant repetition makes it a normal social process. As goods are produced intentionally for exchange, so the concept of exchange-value becomes established as distinct from use-value. And in that process the development of the commodity as the social form assumed by useful objects manifests itself.

As the practice of commodity exchange becomes commonplace and widespread throughout a community, so the quantitative proportion in which commodities are exchangeable becomes dependent on their production, which for Marx is equivalent to the expenditure of as much labour-time as is necessary on average. Thus he refers to the quantitative determination of value by labour-time as a secret hidden under the apparently accidental movements of the exchange-value of commodities (*Capital* 168, 181-2).

Commodity fetishism will also vanish in the fictional world of Robinson Crusoe, which Marx mentions because the tale was a popular one in the classic works of political economy. Crusoe's expenditure of labour-time in the production of useful objects does not have to be considered in his solitary circumstances through the social form of the commodity, and the substitution of such a fantastic form for the simple and transparent relations of Crusoe to his own labour-time and its expenditure on useful objects does not have to take place.

In a feudal society, according to Marx, there is no need for labour and its products to assume a form different from their reality, because the transfer of labour and its products is viewed as the exchange of particular services done by particular workers for superiors to whom they are specifically subordinate. Thus the social relations between individuals involved in the production and transfer of useful goods and services appear 'at all events as their own personal relations, and are not disguised as social relations between things'.

The same is true of the patriarchal peasant family, since the expenditure of an individual's labour-power counts directly as a function of the collective labour of the family according to whatever way labour has been divided up amongst the individual members. Thus the distribution of labour within the family and the expenditure of labour-time by the individuals is not regulated by relations of exchange-value established between the objects they produce. Instead it is regulated directly by the patriarchally enforced distribution of tasks and time that exists within what Marx terms 'directly associated labour'.

Lastly Marx considers a free association of workers, using the means of production in common, and expending their 'different forms of labour-power in full self-awareness as one single social labour force'. This conscious and planned control over production rends the veil of commodity fetishism that in market societies has covered 'the countenance of the social life-process'. Part of the total product of this imagined association, which is one of Marx's sketches of the development of socialism into **communism**, goes towards investment in fresh means of production, whilst another proportion of the product is consumed by members. The social relations of individual producers towards their labour and its products are 'transparent in their simplicity'. The concepts of the commodity, exchange-value and the market do not arise, and the process of production is not regulated by such an indirect mechanism. Instead it is directly regulated by workers themselves (*Capital* 167–73).

In communitarian societies other than socialism or communism, where products of labour do not yet take the form of commodities, workers are largely subordinated to the forces of nature, which they characteristically worship through fetish-gods. Workers in commodity-producing societies, whilst acquiring increasing mastery over natural forces, become subordinate to the market relations established by the exchange of their own products, a process which they characteristically take to be universal amongst humans, inalterably natural and capriciously beneficial or destructive. Such a view, according to Marx, is analogous to the idolatrous worship of nature-gods represented in idol-fetishes, because in both practices people put themselves in the power of their own creations which they then surround with much mystery and superstitious respect.

Both practices arise within an economic **base and super-structure** and correspond to differing levels of development of productive forces. Just as natural forces are personified as the inherent powers of an idol, so the social forces of productive labour are conceptualized as inherent powers of the commodity which manifest themselves when values are realized on the market. Hence the commodity, with its value-in-exchange, is not merely a category of economic analysis, but is in the first instance a concept crucial to the functioning of **capitalism** itself. This is because the commodity functions as a fetish, from which arises a system of market domination and control. That system, in Marx's view, occupies a transitory role in social development, as does the worship of fetish-gods, and both are subject to the critical scrutiny that arises from his hypothesis that the relation of human beings to the natural and social worlds may one day be realized in a way that does not incorporate such fatalism and obscurity.

FURTHER READING

A Marx Dictionary

alienation	ideology
base and superstructure	labour
capitalism	mode of production
communism	science
exploitation	value

Marx's writings
Capital, especially pp. 163–77

Secondary sources
Avineri (1970), especially chapter 4
Callinicos (1983), especially chapter 6
Carver (1982), especially chapter 5
Cohen (1978), especially chapter V
Suchting (1983), especially chapter 13
Wood (1981), especially chapter XV

ideology

A term Marx uses to characterize doctrines or systems of ideas which are not, in his view, scientific. He took over from earlier users of the word the notion that in the social world there are sets of ideas, more or less systematic in characer, which can be adequately isolated for analytical purposes and then subjected to criticism. Marx's criticism does not merely evaluate these systems for descriptive truth or falsity. The notion that his concept of ideology is equivalent to 'false consciousness' was a definition introduced by Engels and never endorsed by Marx, who did not use the phrase.

Whilst Marx proceeds from an assumption that ideas current in society can be distinguished as systems, and then as ideology, he offers no explicit definition. Rather he points to morality, religion, metaphysics, philosophy, the law and political doctrines such as conservatism and liberalism as examples of ideologies. More specifically he uses the term 'ideology' to characterize certain kinds of thinking that may occur even in the course of works which are otherwise scientific. Some works of political economy, the economics of Marx's day, are said to be scientific to the extent that genuine discoveries about the workings of **capitalism** have been established. But they are also said to be ideological when their authors depart in certain ways from what he considers to be the canons of social **science** (*Capital* 95–8, 174–5n).

For Marx ideologies are systems of ideas that are unscientific, not because they incorporate falsehoods (though they may) but because they promulgate illusions, half-truths, misleading arguments, incomplete analyses, unsupported assertions, and implausible premisses. Most importantly they present accounts of social phenomena that serve to promote the interests of individuals or a **class**. Far from being false, the most intellectually and politically important ideologies for Marx are ones that incorporate large measures of truth, plausibility and even genuine scientific information about the social world.

Marx's concept of ideology allows him to attack the works and doctrines of very well-known, influential writers, such as G. W. F. Hegel, Adam Smith, David Ricardo, J. S. Mill, P-J. Proudhon and others, whether conservative, liberal or socialist. It also enables him to dismiss religions, including Christianity and Judaism, as altogether ideological, because he regards any concept of the supernatural as not only false but socially sinister. This is because the gullible may be led by religion to act against their own best interests. Partisan political philosophies, such as divine right of kings, liberal democracy and communitarian socialism, are subject to similar criticisms because they invoke the supernatural, disguise particular interests as the general good or proclaim unrealizable goals. Broad philosophical views, such as idealism, are considered by Marx to be largely ideological, because false or misleading premises about people, society and the general character of reality are used to support political doctrines and programmes that promote the division of society into classes or fail to take the economic causes of that division seriously enough.

In Marx's view all ideologies foster illusions and cast a veil over clear thinking. This happens in ways that have important consequences for the functioning and development of society. Ideologies, which purport to explain politics and the material conditions of life, are not merely unreliable, misleading and apologetic in an intellectual context. Their political functions and implications have to be exposed as well, before scientific thinking founded on Marx's new **materialism** can be substituted. Only then is constructive political action for the transformation of capitalist society into **communism** a real possibility.

Marx's concept of ideology, while not satisfactorily defined, is much more than a pejorative term assigned to writers and movements to which he was politically opposed. It incorporates an implicit distinction between what is scientific and what is not. It focuses on ideas that enable class divisions in society to persist. And it provides a pattern of functional and historical analysis by which doctrinal claims can be evaluated intellectually and politically.

Ideology, for Marx, is a form of social consciousness. Social consciousness, he writes in the 'Preface' of 1859 to *A Contribution to the Critique of Political Economy*, is determined by 'social existence', which necessarily involves production, the 'foundation' or **base** of society, **and** a **superstructure** of legal and political institutions, such as the **state**. He links ideology to social conflicts, which characteristically arise through changes in the economic foundation, and refers to the 'ideological forms of consciousness' through which these conflicts are fought out (*Early Writings* 425–6).

The theory of ideology also appears in Marx's mature work *Capital*, volume 1, of 1867, where he discusses bourgeois consciousness, his term for commonplace beliefs about the capitalist **mode of production**. He relates modern tendencies in Christianity, such as Protestantism and Deism, to recent economic developments in Europe, by suggesting that they incorporate assumptions and doctrines that harmonize with the interests of the bourgeoisie. And he criticizes the specific doctrines, most notably of **value**, price and profit, offered by political economists since the seventeenth century, when he points to the way that their theories purportedly validate political views and policies favouring the capitalist class. While the actual term 'ideology' is not important in these passages, Marx's use of the essential features of his conception is significant, since a good deal of his argument hinges on an identification and criticism of illusions, mysteries and disguised relations in capitalist society whose functioning he summarizes as the **fetishism of commodities**.

Marx never identifies his own ideas as 'Marxism'. Claims that Marxism represents a scientific ideology or a proletarian ideology of **revolution** are at odds with his own use of the term.

FURTHER READING

A Marx Dictionary

base and superstructure	mode of production
capitalism	revolution
class	science
communism	state
fetishism of commodities	value
materialism	

Marx's writings
Capital, especially pp. 163–77

Secondary sources
Callinicos (1983), especially chapter 6
Carver (1982), especially chapter 4
McCarney (1980), especially chapter 1
Mepham (1979c), especially chapters 5–7
Parekh (1982), especially chapters 1, 8
Suchting (1983), especially chapter 14
Wood (1981), especially chapters VIII–X

labour

Perhaps the central concept in Marx's thought, where it performs two related but contrasting functions. As a general concept, human labour is the activity that defines human life itself. This generalization profoundly influences his view of human social development ranging from its earliest prehistoric manifestations to the **communism** that he expects in future. Within contemporary **capitalism** labour is also the sole substance and measure of the **value** of commodities. From that proposition he deduces the necessity of worsening economic crises and the inevitability of proletarian **revolution**.

Marx offers a definition of labour in *Capital*, volume 1, of 1867, that is both general in distinguishing human labour from the activities of animals, and historical in providing a developmental framework within which different human cultures can be located. Building on the presuppositions of his new **materialism** he assumes the existence of human beings as social creatures who are required, by biological necessity, to interact with the material environment of nature. Labour is a process by which people, through their own actions, mediate, regulate and control the interaction between humanity and nature. For Marx labour is an appropriation of what exists in nature for human requirements, the universal condition for the interaction between humans and nature, and the 'everlasting nature-imposed condition of human existence' that is 'common to all forms of society' (*Capital* 290).

What distinguishes human labour from that of animals, 'the worst architect from the best of bees', is the purposive will. Unlike animals, Marx argues, humans have conceptions to which they consciously subordinate their activities for the duration of their work. The subordination of will to purpose, the conscious way in which a preconceived end is realized in practice, and the reflexive character of the human labour process which allows new needs and new activities to develop, all contrast sharply with the instinctive behaviour of animals.

Besides the purposive will, labour requires the use of the body or external tools in order to adapt objects to human needs. Besides natural objects, raw materials may also be objects of labour, but they are simply natural objects which have already undergone some alteration. Thus for Marx the simple elements of the labour process are purposive activity, natural objects and partly worked-up raw materials, and instruments of labour (*Capital* 283–4).

What catches Marx's imagination is not the distinction between human and animal activities but the development of material production in human history. It is not unfair to suggest that for Marx history is essentially an account of this development, since material production is the basis of all social life. While the labour process is an aspect of individual behaviour, the sum and organization of labour in society is the historical process of material production.

For Marx it is variations in the instruments of labour that mark material production as a developmental process, rather than changes in the purposive will or objects of labour and raw materials. Alterations in tools can be observed archaeologically and historically, and he writes that 'relics of bygone instruments of labour possess the same importance for the investigation of extinct economic formations of society as do fossil bones for the determination of extinct species of animals'. For Marx instruments of labour, particularly mechanical ones, provide the standard by which to characterize different social epochs. 'Prehistory has been divided, according to the materials used to make tools and weapons, into the Stone Age, the Bronze Age, and the Iron Age.'

But Marx also suggests that instruments of labour indicate the social relations within which men work. Thus his concept of **mode of production** is founded on two determining factors. One is the materials used to make tools and weapons, e.g. Stone Age, Bronze Age, Iron Age. And the other is the type of social relationships, especially property ownership, within which material production and the distribution of products take place, e.g. slavery, feudalism (*Capital* 284–6).

For Marx development in the labour-process awakens the

'potentialities slumbering within nature', including changes in human nature itself, as different products satisfy human needs and new needs are developed. Thus the history of production is not a mere increase in the productivity of labour, because exactly what counts as labour, what it is expected to accomplish, and the standard or average labour against which increases in output can be measured, all differ from one epoch or mode of production to another.

Very broadly Marx ascribes to all pre-communist modes of production an **alienation** of labour. Alienated labour is itself subject to **exploitation** within some societies when a **class** of owners receives the benefits of labour. Very rudimentary societies in which material production is co-operative and distribution is regulated by need, may avoid exploitation. But in Marx's view, the stimulus to more developed societies is inextricably bound to the benefits derived by an exploiting class from an alteration in the mode of production. Such classes thus overturn old arrangements of production and distribution and introduce new means of production and social relationships, as he suggests in his comments on **base and superstructure**. Rudimentary societies are founded either on human immaturity or on 'direct relations of dominance and servitude'. They are 'conditioned by a low stage of development of the productive powers of labour and correspondingly limited relations' (*Capital* 173, 283).

Thus Marx's apparently economic interpretation of history is the foundation for a political theory of social change, as co-operative, family-based and tribal societies give way to ancient empires and the modern **state**. The non-alienated labour to which he looks forward in communist society is an activity in which the worker enjoys labour as the free play of physical and mental powers (*Capital* 284).

Marx writes in the *Economic and Philosophical Manuscripts* of 1844 that production is the active species life of human beings, because they reproduce themselves intellectually and actually in a world they themselves created. Unlike animals, which produce only when compelled to by physical need and only according to the standards of their own species, humans are 'capable of producing according to the standards of every species and of applying to each object its inherent standard . . . in accordance with the laws of beauty'. More controversially he claims that humans truly produce 'only in freedom from such need', as will be the case under communism when labour will be a spontaneous and free activity. By contrast labour in pre-communist societies is estranged or alienated, because it is a mere means to physical existence. When some work for others, as in class-divided societies, exploitation is heaped on alienation (*Early Writings* 324–30).

Marx pushes his analysis of labour beyond this descriptive and evaluative social **science** in which the featured elements are purposive activity, the object on which work is performed and the instruments used in production. What actually happens when human activity, using the instruments of labour, effects an alteration in an object, is his next concern. From that consideration arise the propositions about labour which underpin his predictions of the economic and political future of capitalist society.

For Marx the worker's activity in using tools to change the form of natural objects or raw materials has certain special properties. Labour is a process 'extinguished in the product'. It 'has become bound up in its object', it has been 'objectified'. The worker's activity then appears in the product as 'a fixed, immobile characteristic'. In a 'successful product, the role played by past labour . . . has been extinguished'.

This argument in *Capital*, volume 1, does two things for Marx. Firstly it establishes a physical, or quasi-physical connection between labouring activity and labour-products such that 'living' or active and 'dead' or objectified labour are equivalent forms of the same substance. They are therefore measurable in principle with respect to some standard unit. And secondly, it excludes 'past labour' – already objectified in partly worked-up raw materials or in instruments of labour – from playing the active role in the labour-process that he assigns exclusively to the 'living labour' exercised by workers. Raw materials and instruments of labour are thus consumed 'in the fire of labour, appropriated as part of its organism, and infused with vital energy' only when living labour awakens them 'from the dead'(*Capital* 287–90).

Marx argues further that however various the activities we identify as labour, 'it is a physiological fact that they are functions of the human organism', and that each function is essentially 'the expenditure of human brain, nerves, muscles, etc.'. From that he deduces an 'abstract' human labour – common to all forms of labouring activity – which can in principle be measured by its duration. He identifies the 'concrete' forms of labour we actually observe as qualitatively different but quantitatively incommensurable, e.g. tailoring and weaving. But he considers the 'abstract' labour common to all forms of labouring activity to be the same in qualitative terms and to be quantitatively measurable as an expenditure of labour-time according to a socially determined unit. This is 'human labour pure and simple' or the 'expenditure of human labour in general'. He also refers to it as simple average labour, which varies in different countries in different epochs but is given in any particular society. He defines it as 'the labour-power possessed in his bodily organism by every ordinary man, on the average, without being developed in any special way' (*Capital* 134–5, 164).

Two more distinctions complete his analysis. One distinction is between labour as an activity and labour-power as the potential to do work. Labour is an expenditure of labour-power, and labour-power is a potential that must be physically replenished within the human subject. This replenishment consists in the means of subsistence, labour-products that in Marx's terms are measurable as so much 'dead' or objectified labour.

Marx argues that the amount of objectified labour required to replenish a worker's labour-power, and the amount of labour the worker can actually perform as that potential is expended, are not necessarily equal. Indeed past labour embodied in the labour-power of a worker may be much less than the living labour the worker can perform. The daily expenditure in work of a worker's labour-power may be considerably more than the daily cost of maintaining it. Marx deduces this from the 'fact that half a day's labour is necessary to keep the worker alive during 24 hours', though the worker goes on to labour a whole day (*Capital* 300–1).

The other distinction is between unskilled and skilled labour, or simple and complex labour. Marx reduces the two to a common commensurability as multiples of the 'simple average labour' that he uses as the common measure for different labouring activities, actual or potential. 'More complex labour counts only as intensified, or rather multiplied simple labour', he writes. This is derived by him from conventional notions of skilled and unskilled occupations. He also argues that skilled labour-power requires a higher input of labour-time to reproduce itself, and he gives an outline of the way this could be calculated (*Capital* 134–5, 274–6, 304–5).

Marx develops this analysis of labour to explain the inter-related phenomena use-value, exchange-value and surplus-value, or in short the basis of the capitalist system in which goods are produced for exchange on the market at a profit accruing to capitalists. He argues that derivations of profit from mere monetary exchange are fallacious. Since this explanation is ruled out, the production process remains the only possible source. Because profit represents an increase in value within a capitalist economy, a self-expanding source for value is required. Labour, for Marx, is self-expanding in the required way, and it also represents the only substance, in his view, that can explain the exchange-value of commodities in the first place, whether they are useful goods, money (as precious metal or coin) or labour-power sold by the hour (*Capital* 258–69).

Marx argues that as different commodities exchange for money, they are brought into relations of equality in terms of value. Those relations can only exist by virtue of some common element. This cannot be 'a geometrical, physical, chemical or other natural property of commodities', because those properties form utility or use-values. As use-values, 'commodities differ above all in quality, while as exchange-values they can differ in quantity'. This is because he defines exchange-value as the purely 'quantitative relation, the proportion in which use-values of one kind exchange for use-values of another kind'. But if use-values are disregarded, as he argues they must be in explaining the purely quantitative relation exchange-value, then only one property remains, 'that of being products of labour'. Commodities are 'merely congealed quantities of homogenous human labour'.

But the value of a commodity is determined socially, for Marx, and not by the individual worker, who might be unskilled or lazy and thus expend more labour on an article than is strictly necessary. Only as much socially average labour counts in the value of a given commodity as is necessary on an average to produce an average sample under normal conditions of production using the average degree of skill and intensity in labour.

There are serious problems of definition with Marx's analysis of labour. The analytical connections between socially average labour and the labour of an ordinary person, and between the total labour-power of society and that of an average unit, are never adequately indicated. Socially necessary labour-time is itself a sliding measure, since it is not the minimum time for production as practised under the most efficient conditions. Rather it is a notional necessity continually eroded as improvements in productivity occur in individual workplaces. Moreover, socially necessary labour-time for Marx also includes the effects of *non-labour* processes on market value, which he translates into statements about changes in socially necessary labour-time. He specifically mentions conditions found in the natural environment as an influence on the labour-time required for the production of a commodity, so that 'the same quantity of labour is present in eight bushels of corn in favourable seasons and in only four bushels in unfavourable seasons.' Consequently more labour is represented in a smaller volume in the second case, so the corn has a greater exchange-value per bushel, even though the actual work done was the same in both years (*Capital* 125–30).

Marx's work on labour stretches credulity at a number of points. Is there a common substance, labour in the abstract, that allows us to define various activities, 'skilled' or 'unskilled', as 'work'? Is a common property in all commodities a necessary condition for establishing their value-in-exchange as represented by the monetary prices with which we are all familiar? Is 'living' labour related to its products as some embodied or objectified substance in the way that he suggests? Can the reproduction costs of workers be calculated in labour-terms? Can the self-expanding character of human labour-power be sustained as a physical or quasi-physical phenomenon?

Marx rightly draws our attention to the exchange-value of goods and services as an artefact produced in society, not some purely physical or extra-social phenomenon. But his claim that value as a social construction functions only because embodied labour-time allows goods to exchange in stable ratios seems highly questionable. Though his theory of the **fetishism of commodities** rightly characterizes the continually varying values of commodities as a 'movement made by things' which control the exchangers, his further claim that labour-time is 'a secret' and 'a regulative law' is debatable (*Capital* 168).

'In all situations', Marx writes, 'the labour-time it costs to produce the means of subsistence must necessarily concern mankind' (*Capital* 164). But to advance from that claim to solving the riddles of money, profits and capital with the 'law of value', he required three further propositions that are difficult to sustain:

1 Human labour is said to be a physiological expenditure of some substance that is uniform and, in principle, measurable.
2 Monetary exchange-ratios are said to be mere fluctuations around a commodity's value.
3 Value is said to be determined by the amount of socially necessary labour-time required in production.

Marx's characterization of human labour as the defining activity of the species is rather more promising. This offers us a view in sharp contrast to the way most modern economics treats labour as a mere factor of production on a par with such non-human factors as land, capital and raw materials. Moreover, his concept of labour as an activity crucial to human fulfilment can be used to highlight the grievances many workers feel when they complain that the conditions of production are inhuman. And it helps us to see that the 'pinch' of unemployment is not merely a reduction in the purchasing power of the consumer nor a simple waste of resources. Labour is arguably the quintessential way that human beings become themselves as individuals within society and is thus an activity that is potentially valuable in itself, not, in principle, mere drudgery. Unemployment is therefore hard for individuals to bear quite apart from material deprivation, because when labour disappears so to some extent do they.

FURTHER READING

A Marx Dictionary

alienation	**materialism**
base and superstructure	**mode of production**
capitalism	**revolution**
class	**science**
communism	**state**
exploitation	**value**
fetishism of commodities	

Marx's writings
Capital, especially pp. 125–37, 163–77, 283–306
Early Writings, 'Economic and Philosophical Manuscripts',
especially pp. 322–34
Grundrisse, especially pp. 83–8

Secondary sources
Avineri (1970), especially chapter 3
Brewer (1984), especially chapters 7–22
Carver (1982), especially chapter 6
Cleaver (1979), especially chapters II–IV
Fine (1975), especially chapter 3
Hodgson (1982), especially part II
Lichtenstein (1983), especially chapter 11
Maguire (1972), especially chapter 4
Mészáros (1972), especially chapter IV
Ollman (1976), especially parts II–III
Roemer (1982), especially chapters 2–3, 5–6
Suchting (1983), especially part III
Walton and Gamble (1972), especially chapters 1, 2, 6
Weeks (1981), especially chapter I
Wood (1981), especially part 1

materialism

A term Marx uses in two different senses:

1 that of existing materialism
2 a new materialism which is his own standpoint.

Marx's criticisms of contemporary society were developed in Prussia in the 1830s and 1840s. In that political context philosophical and theological positions counted for a great deal. This was because the monarchy claimed its right to control opinion by appealing to a distinctly conservative philosophy and theology.

As a critic and self-proclaimed radical Marx felt compelled to distinguish his own views very carefully from competing outlooks, whether conservative or liberal, in order to dispel any suspicion that he differed from others only in detail or that his social criticism was but an unsystematic expression of personal preferences. The more fundamental and systematic his criticism could be, the more powerful its force in politics. Thus his excursions into politics required him to engage with philosophical and theological debates, and for that reason he alluded to the current political contest between materialists and idealists.

Materialism is traditionally a doctrine declaring that all phenomena are ultimately material, and that in particular all ideas have their origin and explanation in a material account of perception. Idealism, by contrast, assigns true or ultimate reality to ideas or concepts which are considered immaterial, and it assigns to thought an active role in determining the truth and reality of experience. The radicals with whom Marx was acquainted variously identified themselves with versions of either materialism or idealism, and his comments on those doctrines reflect this complexity.

In distinguishing himself from conservative and radical

idealists and materialists Marx adopts what he thinks are the minimum necessary presuppositions required for a critical account of contemporary society. He carefully acknowledges his debts to traditional philosophy, but does not claim to have solved all the classic problems. Thus he attacks traditional materialism and idealism, quite apart from their contemporary political guises, as being excessive and erroneous in their claims about experience and knowledge. At the same time he draws attention to elements of each doctrine that conform to the assumptions that he has developed as the foundation for a proper social **science**.

Marx's presuppositions are living human individuals, the material world and human productive activity taking place within it. Traditional debates concerning the ultimate nature of reality (whether material, ideal or both), the relationship between matter and consciousness (whether identical or dual) and the existence or non-existence of God are simply bypassed. Marx identifies himself as a materialist rather than as an idealist because materialism is more commonly identified with atheism, more clearly focused on events in the everyday world, and more closely associated with progress in the natural sciences and technology. Yet in his theses *Concerning Feuerbach* of 1845 he criticizes 'hitherto existing materialism' on four counts. Firstly, it pictures human experience as a process of passive perception and external determinism. Secondly, it presents the standards by which we judge truth and falsity as a set of theoretical or scientific protocols. Thirdly, it sanctions elitism by appealing to expert knowledge. And fourthly, it treats human beings as if they could be abstracted from their full social context.

In some respects, Marx comments in his theses on Feuerbach, idealists have done a better job. They are more likely to assume that human experience is an active process in which a human world is created, albeit pre-eminently in ideas. They recognize that standards of truth and falsity alter as experience progresses. And they see human experience as essentially and necessarily social, even to the creation of the individual as a personality that can be developed only through interaction with others.

Against both doctrines Marx offers an account of human experience as neither simply material nor ultimately intellectual. Rather he suggests its essence is 'practical, human sensuous activity', most importantly that of productive **labour**. For Marx it is labour that unites human individuals in their 'ensemble' of social relations, and thus he rejects materialist accounts which assume an 'isolated' individual and a mere 'dumb generality' uniting individuals. Thus the standpoint of his 'new' materialism is 'social humanity'.

In contrast to traditional materialist and idealist philosophies Marx's new materialism introduces an anti-elitism when he makes the 'human essence' turn on practical, labouring activities. In determining truth, materialists look to scientists and idealists look to philosophers. Marx announces that 'objective truth' is a 'practical question'. Moreover in changing society he looks to a 'revolutionary practice' founded on the coincidence 'of the changing of circumstances and of human activity', thus forestalling idealist elitism (where intellectuals and 'great men' make history), and materialist psychologies (which do not take history into account) (*Early Writings* 421–3).

Marx considers materialists to be carelessly unhistorical and idealists unwarrantedly teleological. He views human experience as a developmental process but one founded in socially sustained changes in the **mode of production**, hence alterations in the **base and superstructure** of society, an overall process of **revolution**. Thus his presuppositions – living individuals, their activity, the material world – are the ones he needs to generate a politics that is democratic insofar as it takes human beings to be quintessentially workers. For that reason it is readily identified with the working **class**, which he regards as particularly disadvantaged and therefore uniquely capable of overthrowing **capitalism** and establishing **communism**.

To distinguish himself from traditional materialists and idealists, Marx comments again on his outlook or standpoint in *Capital*, volume 1, of 1867. He identifies his method as 'materialist', in that he works from 'actual, given relations of life' in order to unmask the **ideology** into which this reality has been 'apotheosized'. 'Actual given relations' are located by him in the 'actual relation of man to nature' as revealed by the technology used in the 'direct process of production'. This is a 'material basis' which includes the 'historical process'. Thus idealists are those who work from 'misty' ideologies to a misunderstanding of social relations in their philosophy, and 'abstract' materialists

are those who work from individualistic psychologies to knowledge that lacks social context (*Capital* 493–4).

Marx's work in *Capital*, volume 1, emphasizes the historical
development of production and particularly the important part
played by scientific knowledge in the evolution of modern
capitalism. But the controversial arguments in the work are
those which rely, as Marx admits, on a **dialectic** derived from
Hegel the arch-idealist.

The arguments in question are the highly abstract propositions which present capitalism as an ideal or conceptual system.
This is an apparently a priori construction in which the life of the
subject-matter is reflected in ideas. In turn, this is based on an
analysis of existing social circumstances, Marx says, and only
after that work has been done can his results be presented in a
way that makes clear the inner structure of the social phenomenon most in question – capital.

Marx's presentation of the dialectic is a specification of the
'active side' developed in idealist philosophy, in which human
history, development, change, fluidity, contradiction and even
negation or destruction are emphasized. These are all a far cry,
in his mind, from the unchanging truths sought by materialists.
This active side is merely mystical when it seems 'to transfigure
and glorify what exists', as he claims it does in Hegel's works. In
the rational form in which Marx uses it, however, it is 'in essence
critical and revolutionary', an analytical tool that exposes the
conceptual bases of the class conflicts that he perceives in
society. In any case, his new materialism is exactly opposite to
Hegel's idealism in its presuppositions about human subjects,
their productive activities both material and intellectual, and
their material and historical setting. Hegel's mystificatory
presuppositions – that thinking or 'the Idea' is itself an active
subject and the creator of the real world – made it easy for him to
present a transfiguration and glorification of contemporary
institutions, because he looked towards abstract intellectual
achievement. Marx looks to a universal material fulfilment for
real people. This was the basis of his political criticism of the
contemporary world (*Capital* 102–3).

Marx's new materialism bears a complex and critical relationship to other materialisms, even radical ones, and to the idealism
which dominated the German political and intellectual environ-

ment in which he grew up. The 'historical', 'dialectical' and 'scientific' materialisms with which he has been commonly identified have their origins in the work of Engels. One should not assume a coincidence between Marx's views and those attributed to him by Engels, because the propositions of 'historical materialism' and 'materialist' dialectics as formulated by Engels arguably contradict Marx's carefully circumscribed new materialism.

FURTHER READING

A Marx Dictionary
base and superstructure   **ideology**
capitalism   **labour**
class   **mode of production**
communism   **revolution**
dialectic   **science**

Marx's writings
Capital, especially pp. 94–103
Early Writings, 'Economic and Philosophical Manuscripts', especially pp. 383–400, 421–3

Secondary sources
Avineri (1970), especially chapter 4
Callinicos (1983), especially chapters 4–5
Carver (1982), especially chapter 3
Mepham (1979b), especially chapters 1–3
Norman (1980), especially chapters 4–5
Ruben (1979), especially chapters III–V
Sayer (1979), especially chapter 5
Suchting (1983), especially chapter 4
Walton and Gamble (1972), especially chapter 3
Wood (1981), especially chapters V, VII, VIII and part 4

mode of production

A term Marx uses in his new **materialism**. The concept 'mode of production' allows him to distinguish between different kinds of societies or 'social formations' that have existed in human history, and to analyse different kinds of production within a given society. The most famous treatment of it in his work is in the 'Preface' of 1859 to *A Contribution to the Critique of Political Economy*. His statement that the mode of production of material life conditions the general process of social, political and intellectual life is arguably the most concise expression of his outlook that we have. It seems to summarize the more specific claims he makes concerning the 'relations of production' – into which people inevitably enter as they produce their material means of life in society – and the 'forces of production' to which those relations are said by him to correspond.

The term 'forces of production' covers the technological basis for economic activity – tools, machines, energy sources – and the term 'relations of production' refers to the network of social roles encompassing the use and ownership of productive forces and of the products that emerge. Examples of relations of production in capitalist society are employer, wage-worker, investor, dependant, unemployed person and so forth.

According to Marx, relations of production correspond historically and functionally to current forces of production, and those relations constitute the economic structure of society, a real foundation or **base**. On that foundation arises a legal **and** political **superstructure** – the legal relations and political forms of the **state**.

In the 'Preface' of 1859 Marx refers 'in broad outline' to 'the Asiatic, ancient, feudal and modern bourgeois modes of production'. Those, he says, are 'epochs marking progress in the economic development of society' (*Early Writings* 425–6).

The modern bourgeois mode of production is at the heart of

Marx's intellectual and political activity. In the *Communist Manifesto* of 1848 he writes that 'the bourgeoisie, during its rule of scarce of one hundred years', has created colossal productive forces, subjugating nature and introducing machinery, agricultural science, steam engines, canals and 'whole populations conjured out of the ground'. In doing so it destroys established industries and ways of life and replaces old wants by new demands throughout the world (*Revolutions* 71, 72). And in *Capital*, volume 1, of 1867, he says that the bourgeois mode of production is essentially revolutionary, because the forces of production are continually transformed, and so are the 'functions of the worker and the social combinations of the **labour** process'. Earlier modes are 'essentially conservative' (*Capital* 617).

The other modes of production mentioned by Marx do not have this character, because they do not incorporate a drive towards continual alteration in the forces of production. Thus technological change in pre-capitalist modes of production comes more slowly than in the recent industrial development in Europe, which was his major interest. In his view a difference in the forces of production and in their rate of development distinguishes the bourgeois mode of production from its predecessors.

For Marx it is not differences in the forces of production that seem to distinguish the Asiatic, ancient and feudal modes of production from each other, nor does he point exclusively to such differences when distinguishing those forms from the modern bourgeois mode. Rather in *Capital*, volume 1, he comments that what distinguishes the various economic formations of society – for example a society based on slave-labour (the ancient mode of production) from one based on wage-labour (the modern bourgeois mode) – is the social relation of production by which an economic surplus is extracted from the immediate producer for the benefit of a ruling **class**.

Feudal society is presented by Marx as a set of customary and legal obligations falling most heavily on serfs who provide stated amounts of compulsory labour for their lords, tithes to priests and personal services to those higher in the social hierarchy. Thus the feudal mode of production is also distinguished in that non-technological way from fully-fledged slavery and from wage-labour in modern **capitalism** (*Capital* 170–1, 325).

Amongst communal forms of production, where the conditions of production are owned or managed by communities or
primitive states, Marx identifies village communes in India and
indeed the earliest beginnings of co-operative labour, dating
back to hunting peoples and family-based agriculture. In this
Asiatic or communal mode of production he sees the worker as
being wholly subordinate to the community organization, rather
than enslaved as in the ancient mode of production, or
subordinate to particular persons as in feudalism, or free of such
traditional obligations, as in modern bourgeois society. Again,
non-technological factors distinguish one mode of production
from another.

But Marx also offers a contrasting technological account of
modes of production, arguing in *Capital*, volume 1, that it is
forces of production that distinguish different economic epochs
from each other. He strongly endorses the division of prehistory
into the Stone Age, Bronze Age and Iron Age. Instruments of
labour, especially mechanical ones, identify the degree of
economic development and alter the social relations within
which work takes place (*Capital* 285–6).

We know very little about social relations in prehistory, and
Marx's thesis is not much more than an assertion. Moreover he
does not investigate the way that the three epochs – Stone,
Bronze, Iron – can be correlated with tools that are significantly
different from each other in some mechanical way, and we are
not told how this prehistorical progression is related to the
Asiatic or communal, ancient and feudal modes of production
that feature in historical times.

Marx uses forces of production as his defining criterion
somewhat ineffectively for prehistory and then more successfully
for the obvious developments in technology that he associates
with the rise of the bourgeoisie in Europe and with the bourgeois
mode of production. This last historical and economic development is the only one where his two criteria – forces and relations
of production – coincide convincingly in distinguishing one
mode of production from another.

Marx considers three transitions amongst his modes of
production – ancient to feudal, feudal to bourgeois, and
bourgeois to communist. He gives credit to military and cultural

explanations for the fall of the Roman Empire, the last ancient civilization in the West. His account of the feudal relations of production which followed it makes them convincingly different from classical societies based on slave-labour. But he does not really compare the forces of production in the two societies – ancient and feudal – nor does he explain in terms of a correspondence of relations of production to forces of production why ancient and feudal societies should be so different.

Marx's view that the transition from feudal to modern bourgeois society involves a conflict between newly developing forces of production and entrenched feudal relations of production has historical plausibility. This conflict is being resolved, he writes, in an era of social **revolution** in which the whole immense superstructure of feudal relations in the law and politics is being transformed. The feudal classes – agents of technological and social conservatism – and bourgeois classes – agents of technological and social revolution – are coming into conflict as new forces and new corresponding relations of production are developing in society.

Marx forecasts a process of revolution as modern bourgeois society gives way to socialism and **communism**. While he suggests a conflict between existing forces and relations of production in capitalist society, his account of this conflict does not depend on rapid development in the forces of production themselves, as his account of the previous transition from feudal to bourgeois society had done. He suggests that bourgeois relations of production are becoming a fetter on any further technological development, but argues that communism can be built on the technological legacy of the bourgeoisie.

The four historical modes of production – Asiatic or communal, ancient, feudal and modern bourgeois – and the three prehistorical modes – Stone, Bronze and Iron – are not delineated as successfully as they might be in Marx's social **science**. This is because forces, relations and modes of production are not distinctly and consistently related to each other and to the concepts of economic structure and economic foundation or base. Moreover his various comments on the way that different modes of production can be distinguished from each other are not demonstrably consistent. Sometimes he appeals to forces of production as the distinguishing factor and at other times to relations of production. In considering transitions from one mode of production to another he points in certain cases to forces of production as the crucial factor in historical change and in other cases to relations of production, without explaining why he shifts from one to the other. But the importance he assigns to production itself in any consideration of social life and social change – prehistorical, historical, contemporary and future – has been almost universally conceded.

FURTHER READING

A Marx Dictionary
base and superstructure   **materialism**
capitalism   **revolution**
class   **science**
communism   **state**
labour

Marx's writings
Capital, especially pp. 170–1, 285–7, 425, 452–3
Grundrisse, especially pp. 471–514
Revolutions, 'Communist Manifesto', especially pp. 67–87

Secondary sources
Bloch (1984), especially chapters 1–3
Carver (1982), especially chapter 3
Cohen (1978), especially chapters III, VI–VII
Sawer (1977), especially chapters I, II, V
Shaw (1978), especially chapters 1–3
Turner (1978), especially chapters 1, 5
Wood (1981), especially chapter V

revolution

Marx first published an explicit call to European revolution in his *A Contribution to the Critique of Hegel's 'Philosophy of Right'. Introduction* of 1844. He was just twenty-five years old when he wrote it.

In contemporary political terms the French Revolution of 1789 was still a recent event, and conservatives and liberals interpreted it very differently. German conservatives regarded with extreme suspicion any moves to establish representative and responsible parliamentary government, freedoms of the press, person and religion and the political equality of all citizens – 'the rights of man and the citizen'. They viewed these as inherently revolutionary, rather than merely liberal, because they thought that representative democracy would threaten their authoritarian kingdoms and feudal political structures. For that reason they associated liberal ideas and representative democracy with mass uprisings and violence.

The Rhenish newspaper of which Marx was briefly editor in 1842 and 1843 published articles that endorsed liberal political ideas. Marx, however, came to identify himself with **communism**, which he saw as the movement to abolish private property in productive resources by means of a working-class revolution.

From 1844 onwards Marx argues that radical politics must move beyond a liberal view of persons as citizens to an analysis of society in terms of social **class**. The proletarian or working class, he writes, is a new social creation, a product of the emerging industrial system **capitalism**, which is founded on the laws of private property that allows owners of industry to accumulate profits. These are derived from goods produced by labourers who are inevitably poorly rewarded. Thus in his view, the working class stands in all-sided opposition to the developing political system in Germany (*Early Writings* 256).

Marx identifies the proletarian movement in principle with communism, and his political activity proceeds on that basis. His politics is by definition revolutionary, because it contradicts the very principles of both liberals and conservatives. He comments that Germany has 'shared the restorations of modern nations without ever having shared their revolutions' (*Early Writings* 245).

Marx distinguishes between merely political revolutions, which leave the economic pillars of society still standing, and the radical revolution of universal human emancipation which he expects from communist revolutionary action. In the eighteenth century, he argues, it was possible for all disadvantaged classes in society to identify politically with 'the rights of man and the citizen'. But in an economy based on private property in productive resources, only those with money and education would eventually benefit in practice.

In the French Revolution middle-class opposition to the nobility and clergy made the bourgeoisie appear to all the lower social classes as liberators casting out the reactionary forces of oppression. But in the nineteenth century, Marx claims that this is not possible any more, since 'the rights of man and the citizen' are no longer credible as a form of liberation for the masses in industrial society. Indeed, the sufferings of industrial workers are not, according to Marx, mere class disadvantages, but are instead a manifestation of 'wrong in general' and the 'total loss of humanity'. Thus the proletariat is not so much a class as 'the dissolution of all classes', and its position as a representative of 'universal suffering' derives from the ultimate **alienation** of **labour** that it experiences.

Marx writes that the proletariat 'proclaims the dissolution of the existing world order', since the 'secret of its own existence' is the 'actual dissolution of that order' (*Early Writings* 256–7). His subsequent critical work on political economy, culminating in *Capital*, volume 1, of 1867, aims to show why the interests of proletarians and bourgeoisie are incompatible within capitalism and why that system is subject to inevitable economic crises. He indicates, in rough outline, how an alternative communist system, which will emancipate all humanity from **exploitation**, can be constructed.

'Let the ruling classes tremble at a communistic revolution',

Marx writes in the *Communist Manifesto* of 1848, 'the proletarians have nothing to lose but their chains.' Within this overall schema one major problem is the timing of the two revolutions – bourgeois and proletarian – in countries other than England and France, which have already, in his view, experienced bourgeois revolutions. In the 1840s he turned his attention to Germany, partly because as a Prussian he had an entrée into German politics, but also, as he announces in the *Communist Manifesto*, because Germany is 'on the eve of a bourgeois revolution'. In his opinion this will be 'but the prelude to an immediately following proletarian revolution'.

However, Marx does not describe the exact character of proletarian revolution, in contrast to certain aspects of the bourgeois revolution which he urges workers to support and which he stipulates in some detail. Those details include the abolition of property in land, a graduated income tax, abolition of the right of inheritance, confiscation of the property of emigrants and rebels, centralization of credit by means of a national bank, state ownership of factories, equal liability of all to labour, merger of agricultural and manufacturing industry, and free education for all children in public schools (*Revolutions* 86–7, 98).

Marx's view on how the 'immediately following' proletarian revolution is to be fought are revealed in the context of the counter-revolutionary politics that prevailed over the next two decades. In his 'Address of the Central Committee to the Communist League' of March 1850 he writes that proletarians are ultimately 'to make the revolution permanent' by driving out the propertied classes from their ruling position. But his time-scale for this struggle lengthens as revolutionary enthusiasm dwindles. In particular, he predicts that German workers can expect a 'protracted revolutionary development', but one that will be accelerated by the 'direct victory of their own class in France' (*Revolutions* 323, 330).

After the failure of the liberal uprisings of 1848 and 1849 Marx outlines a view of proletarian revolution that is less optimistic than the one in the *Communist Manifesto*. In *The Eighteenth Brumaire of Louis Bonaparte*, a work on contemporary French politics published in 1852, he says that such revolutions suffer 'repeated interruptions'. They 'engage in self-criticism', they 'return to what has apparently already been accomplished in order to begin the task again', they 'seem to throw their opponent to the ground only to see him draw new strength'. Their opponents 'rise again before them, more colossal than ever.'

Bourgeois revolutions, by contrast, 'storm quickly from success to success', because opposition to the aristocracy unifies all other classes. But bourgeois revolutions are short-lived and society must endure a restoration in order to assimilate soberly the achievements of its period of 'storm and stress'. Proletarian revolutions, in Marx's view, will have no such successes to rely on, because opposition to the bourgeoisie does not ally all other classes so firmly with the proletariat. This is because all non-proletarian classes have some sort of stake in bourgeois society to defend. The proletariat can achieve victory only when further retreat for it is impossible (*Surveys* 150).

Marx's view of revolutionary struggle takes account of strong counter-revolutionary forces in the very societies from which he expects proletarian uprisings. Indeed they are not the societies where capitalism is most advanced and where propertied classes are the strongest. That honour goes to Britain, which he takes as the main illustration of the capitalist **mode of production**, since it is the national economy where this phenomenon occurs in its purest state, but he was not optimistic about a British revolution (*Capital* 90).

Thus Marx's theory of revolution is not tied directly to a theory of *national* economic development. He looks consistently for revolution in countries where capitalist industry is newly introduced, where capitalist classes are not yet strong and where feudal classes, especially peasants, are still preponderant in the population as a whole. According to this view Germany, France and eventually Russia become weak points in the international development of capitalist industry. Proletarians, in uneasy alliance with the bourgeoisie or middle classes, may be able to exploit political weakness and signal the working class in more industrialized countries such as Britain that communist revolution is possible. In that way his theory of revolution is compatible with a theory of the economic and political development of *international* capitalism.

Shortly after the Paris Commune of 1871, in which ordinary

Parisians rebelled against the conservative republicans who succeeded the Emperor Napoleon III, Marx published *The Civil War in France*. In that work he evaluates the Commune as a prototype of proletarian revolution and comments that the working class 'did not expect miracles'. There will have to be 'long struggles', even 'historic processes', before they can 'set free the elements of the new society with which old collapsing bourgeois society itself is pregnant'. He hints that the Commune was afflicted with an unavoidable evil in the form of poor leaders, 'mere bawlers' and worse, who 'hampered the real action of the working class'. He concludes that the Commune did not have time to shake them off before it was bloodily suppressed (*First International* 213, 219).

In the early 1880s Marx addresses the circumstances of Russian radicals and self-professed revolutionaries fighting the most reactionary regime in Europe. In his brief and somewhat enigmatic remarks he does not rule out the possibility of a communist revolution based on peasant communes, provided it becomes the prelude to proletarian revolution in the industrialized countries of Europe.

Marx's comments on revolution in the modern world presuppose political activity, violent and non-violent, rather than simple economic determinism. He acknowledges in an 1872 'Speech on the Hague Congress' of the International Working Men's Association that there are prospects for peaceful revolution in countries such as the United States of America, Britain and The Netherlands. In those countries institutions, customs and traditions may temper the power-struggle between bourgeoisie and proletariat (*First International* 324).

It is not easy to reconcile Marx's many comments on actual and potential revolutionary situations with the much more schematic and stirring pronouncements for which he is famous. In his 'Preface' of 1859 to *A Contribution to the Critique of Political Economy* he writes in general terms that 'at a certain stage of development, the material productive forces of society come into conflict with the existing relations of production', and more specifically with the property relations within which they have previously functioned. Those relations, he continues, are thus changed from forms in which productive forces develop to forms in which further development is checked or fettered, and 'then begins an era of social revolution'. In studying such an era, however, he argues that a transformation in the material conditions of production can be traced more precisely than transformations in the **ideology** that surrounds actual political conflicts as individuals fight them out (*Early Writings* 425–6).

In *Capital*, volume 1, Marx theorizes in a similar way. As the number of capitalists decreases, and their monopoly of the advantages of industrial society develops, so grows the revolt of the working class. 'The monopoly of capital becomes a fetter upon the mode of production', and 'the centralization of the means of production and the socialization of labour' become incompatible with the defining premisses of capitalist society, including private property in productive resources, **value** and money. 'The knell of capitalist private property sounds', and 'the expropriators are expropriated' (*Capital* 929).

Thus in Marx's **science** a schematic account of revolutionary development within capitalism – founded on a study of the material conditions of production – coexists with a more fluid and sometimes less optimistic account of contemporary revolutionary politics – founded on a study of actual political conflicts. For Marx revolution was on the one hand a deduction from his economic analysis of class society and on the other a real phenomenon to be encouraged in prospect and evaluated in retrospect. His economic deductions provided the basis from which that encouragement and evaluation proceeded.

FURTHER READING

A Marx Dictionary

alienation	ideology
capitalism	labour
class	mode of production
communism	science
exploitation	value

Marx's writings
Capital, especially pp. 929–30
Early Writings, 'Introduction' (1844), especially pp. 243–57;
'Economic and Philosophical Manuscripts', especially pp. 424–8
First International, 'Civil War in France', especially pp. 206–21;
'Speech on the Hague Congress', especially p. 324
Revolutions, 'Communist Manifesto', especially pp. 62–87, 97–8;
'Address of Central Committee' (March 1850), especially pp.
323–4
Surveys, 'Eighteenth Brumaire', especially pp. 143–56

Secondary sources
Avineri (1970), especially chapters 5–8
Carver (1982), especially chapter 4
Gilbert (1981), especially parts 1–3
Maguire (1978), especially chapter 2–5
Ollman (1976), especially chapter 5
Suchting (1983), especially chapter 3 and part IV

science

The usual translation of the German *Wissenschaft*, which refers to disciplined study in any field. Marx was not accustomed to making a sharp distinction between arts and science in subject-matter or method. Instead he treated subjects such as philosophy, anthropology, political theory and experimental and natural sciences as distinguishable but related branches of knowledge. Study in those disciplines presupposed some common factors in methodology, but allowed for variation in method as required. His discussion of the relationship between those different areas of human knowledge is an interesting one, because it bears on the way that we read his work and on the way that we conceive the non-human, human and social aspects of the world.

Marx's view of the world rests on three presuppositions – living individuals, their productive activity or **labour** and their material environment. He sees human development as the practical process by which everyday, material industry transforms the conditions and practices of social life. With that transformation comes the progressive awakening of human powers that we call civilization. For Marx the modern human is to a large extent a self-created creature, and even the human senses are properly conceived as products of historical development.

Marx's conception of human needs and intellect presupposes that nature has a human essence, because he sees it as the material basis of artefacts. Humans have a natural essence, because their productive activity, which transforms them, is a response to physical needs. The traditional distinction between human life and nature is thus reconceptualized by Marx as a historical process of self-transformation.

Marx argues that this practical transformation is accomplished by humans as self-developing agents. But self-development in history is not a smoothly progressive process. Productive activity under **capitalism** unwittingly produces dehumanization or **alienation**, whilst preparing the conditions for human emancipation under **communism**.

Marx's conception of natural science presupposes that science is a form of practical intervention in human life through industry. Natural science for Marx is much more than a body of merely theoretical knowledge. 'Industry', he writes in the *Economic and Philosophical Manuscripts* of 1844, 'is the real historical relationship . . . of natural science' to human beings.

Thus when Marx concludes that 'sense perception . . . must be the basis of all science' he does two things. Firstly he replaces individualistic non-historical theories of sense perception with a view of the senses as belonging to individuals but developing historically in society. Secondly he replaces the theory that science is merely an accurate record of sense perception with the view that science is an activity presupposing human industry as well as intellect.

Human history, the transformation of nature and human beings by industry, is for Marx 'a real part of natural history' and an object of scientific inquiry just as much as natural objects. But inquiry into natural objects also presupposes for Marx the intimate relation between those objects and the human activity that he sees as the basis of industry. He sums this up when he writes that 'natural science will in time subsume the science of man just as the science of man will subsume natural science' (*Early Writings* 354–5).

Marx's conclusion is not that the study of human beings should be part of the natural sciences as traditionally conceived. That traditional conception he describes as 'abstractly material or rather idealist', because it does not presuppose the facts about individuals, productive activity and the material environment that are required by his new **materialism**.

Nor does Marx conclude that the incorporation of natural science into a humanistic philosophical framework is enough, since he describes this approach as 'a fantastic illusion'. Rather he proposes a radical transformation in the way that natural science is conceived as an activity, and in the way that human beings are regarded when they develop and employ scientific knowledge (*Early Writings* 315).

Natural science is not rationalized and validated philosophically by Marx in the manner of Hegel, nor is social science recast as a study arising from premises about matter as it is treated by the natural sciences. Marx's conception of science is founded instead on a view about human needs and intellect as they develop in practical life, not on propositions about the general nature of everything, whether ultimately material or otherwise.

Marx breaks with traditional conceptions of natural and social science, since he does not ally himself either with materialists, who reduce the social to the material, or with idealists, who admit the material world only as part of the world of ideas. He assumes instead one science that presupposes a transformative and self-transformative continuity between humans and the material world, without specifying that continuity as something which is ultimately either material or intellectual in character. On that point he is agnostic, so he bypasses the debates about the ultimate nature of reality that are for him a distraction from the politics of contemporary capitalist society. His conception of science allows this agnosticism, because for him science is a practical activity that arises out of this continuity and confirms it as the key to a pattern of social development in which one **mode of production** succeeds another.

Science for Marx is not a matter of mere 'enlightenment, utility and a few great discoveries' but rather an element in the practical transformation of human life through industry, something that traditional historiography has neglected (*Early Writings* 355). Science therefore has a direct relationship to the economic structure of society or **base and** an indirect one to the **superstructure**. Arising from the economic foundation or base is a superstructure of legal and political institutions. Ideas about those institutions are social consciousness. For Marx social consciousness includes scientific theory and its opposite **ideology**.

Marx identifies as ideological three views in the consciousness of contemporary society that are relevant to his view of science. First, there are presuppositions about natural science that occur in the traditional conceptions of idealists or materialists. He suggests that they treat science as a record of truth isolated from contemporary social experience, in particular industry and technology. Second, there are presuppositions about scientists held by philosophers. These are ideological because philosophers take scientists to be disinterested seekers after truth. Third, some of the work of contemporary social scientists is ideological, because what they say about society is misleading, incompletely argued, self-serving or in the interests of a particular **class**.

In establishing his own work on society as scientific Marx undertook a revision of the term 'science' itself, and a revision of the way that human beings, their relations in society and their social development are regarded. Those revisions did not in themselves establish the scientific method by which his critical work on capitalist society proceeds, any more than they dictate a methodology in any other scientific study.

Marx is acutely conscious that the basis of his chosen subject, the workings of capitalist society, is purposive behaviour which arises from concepts held by individuals. Thus for him human behaviour is a phenomenon rooted in concepts, and a large measure of his social science is therefore conceptual analysis that clarifies behaviour and identifies conflicting interests or 'contradictions' in society.

The method of inquiry in social science, Marx generalizes in his 'Introduction' of 1857 to the *Grundrisse*, is to find an 'inner connection' or structural relationship between concepts, for example capital and **exploitation**. He does this by breaking down the complicated concepts he associates with everyday experience and observation, for example the **state** and competition. To understand those concepts he analyses rudimentary abstractions, such as division of labour, money and **value** (*Grundrisse* 100–1). Working back to the level of everyday observation from this basis is his method of presentation. Marx's social science requires both processes – analysing everyday observation for constituent abstractions, and advancing from the level of abstraction back to that of ordinary experience. In *Capital*, volume 1, of 1867, he writes that his work mirrors the 'life of the subject matter' in ideas so that the finished account has the appearance of an a priori construction (*Capital* 102).

Marx's science admits the importance of sensory observation, but requires its analysis in terms of abstractions. Some of those abstractions may refer to things which the senses themselves cannot perceive. He compares his 'scientific analysis of competition', which requires him to specify the 'inner nature of capital', with the way that astronomy made intelligible the 'apparent motions of the heavenly bodies' by giving an account of their 'real motions, which are not perceptible to the senses'. To do that, astronomers required certain abstract concepts such as 'mass', 'velocity' and 'acceleration', and it is not far-fetched to see Marx's abstract concepts 'commodity' and 'labour' performing a similar function in his summation of the 'motion' of capitalist society as a **fetishism of commodities** (*Capital* 433).

Marx's use of a **dialectic** or specification of social contradictions does not commit him to any general 'laws' underlying all phenomena. Nor do his comparisons of his own method to that of natural scientists commit him to their materialist premises or to all their methods. He likens his efforts in examining the capitalist mode of production to the work of physicists who observe 'natural processes where they occur in their most significant form' and 'are least affected by disturbing influences'. In 'the analysis of economic forms', he writes, 'neither microscopes nor chemical reagents are of assistance'. The 'power of abstraction', he concludes, 'must replace both'. (*Capital* 90).

Marx had a careful and critical appreciation of the presuppositions and methods of natural scientists that was quite as acute as his work on philosophers. Because philosophers had commented on natural science, his critical work on science was to some extent, though not exclusively, conducted through a critical examination of philosophical doctrines. Philosophers since his time have been slow to recognize the truly radical way in which traditional debates have been thrust aside by Marx and traditional distinctions provocatively reconceptualized.

Scientists who believe that the relationship of their intellectual work to other activities in society ought to be considered and influenced by scientists themselves and by the public at large can cite a clear justification for this position in Marx's concept of science, where the work of the 'expert' is put very firmly into a social and political context. Within that context we find the economic and political activities in society that allow scientific work to proceed and that make industrial and technological reality out of its discoveries. There we have the real process of material and social transformation which, so Marx warns us, is reshaping our world and ourselves.

FURTHER READING

A Marx Dictionary

alienation	**fetishism of commodities**
base and superstructure	**ideology**
capitalism	**labour**
class	**materialism**
communism	**mode of production**
dialectic	**state**
exploitation	**value**

Marx's writings
Capital, especially pp. 89–103
Early Writings, 'Economic and Philosophical Manuscripts',
especially pp. 348–58
Grundrisse, especially pp. 100–8

Secondary sources
Carver (1982), especially chapter 3
Cohen (1978), especially chapters IX–X; Appendix I
Maguire (1972), especially chapter 6
Mepham (1979b), especially chapters 2–4
Mepham (1979c), especially chapters 3–4
Parekh (1982), especially chapter 8
Ruben (1979), especially chapters III–V
Sayer (1979), especially part II
Walton and Gamble (1972), especially chapter 3
Wood (1981), especially chapter VIII and part 5

state

The subject of the fourth book in Marx's projected study of 'bourgeois economy', the economic system of **capitalism**. The complete series, as he sketched it in his 'Preface' of 1859 to *A Contribution to the Critique of Political Economy*, was to have consisted of studies of capital, landed property, wage-**labour**, then the state, foreign trade and world market. Only the first of several projected volumes for the first study was published during Marx's lifetime, and it appeared in 1867 as *Capital*, volume 1.

Marx resists all presuppositions or doctrines that present political activity, citizenship and rulership – in short the state – as something quite separate from the productive processes of ordinary economic life in modern society. Following a common convention he refers to the latter as 'civil society' or 'bourgeois society' (both translations of the German *bürgerliche Gesellschaft*).

Marx argues that the state must be considered in conjunction with civil society, generalizing in his 'Preface' of 1859 that 'the **mode of production** of material life conditions the general process of social, political and intellectual life.' On the economic **base** of society, he writes, arises a legal **and** political **superstructure**, clearly his terms for the state and the social phenomena we associate with it (*Early Writings* 425–6).

Those concepts and insights appear at an early stage in Marx's writings. In his *On the Jewish Question* of 1844 he criticizes liberal views that the two spheres – the bourgeois economy and the modern state – could co-exist in such a way that freedom, utility or justice could be maximized. In making this claim he argues that liberals reduce people on the one hand to the real egoism of individuals in civil society and on the other to ideally moral citizens with no real existence. Thus in a liberal state people regard themselves as communal beings united in a political community, but their real life in the world of civil society is in sharp contrast. People are active in the real world of civil society as private individuals who treat others as mere means to their own selfish ends, and all become the victims of **alienation** and **class** struggle (*Early Writings* 229–34).

Because people live in a real world of cut-throat competition, Marx claims in the *Communist Manifesto* of 1848 that in modern societies political power 'is merely the organized power of one class for oppressing another', and he remarks that 'the executive of the modern state is but a committee for managing the common affairs of the whole bourgeoisie' (*Revolutions* 69, 87).

Marx's comments on the state pose two major problems. First, to what extent and in what ways are existing states conditioned by the capitalist mode of production? And second, what forms of proletarian rule may supplant the states, liberal or otherwise, that currently exist?

While Marx claims that a legal and political superstructure rises from the economic structure of society, and that the mode of production of material life conditions political life, he never denies the counter-influence of the state on the economic aspects of society. Indeed he writes extensively about one case, the military dictatorship that succeeded the Second Republic of 1848 to 1851 in France. In *The Eighteenth Brumaire of Louis Bonaparte* of 1852 he argues that Bonaparte's state does not correspond to the economic structure. He even concludes that the state seems to have attained a completely autonomous position with respect to civil society.

In French civil society of the Second Republic, according to Marx, the bourgeoisie was the ruling class, but the dictator Bonaparte was not their instrument, nor their representative, as certain previous rulers had been, the 'July Monarch' King Louis Philippe in particular. Louis Bonaparte broke the power of the middle class and saw himself, according to Marx, as the opponent of their political and literary power. He represented the conservative peasantry, the state bureaucracy, the church and the army.

Marx portrays a tension between Bonaparte's power base in the peasantry and the true strength of the country in the business affairs of the middle class. Thus the apparent exception to his generalization concerning the relationship of base and super-structure allows him to diagnose a potential conflict of interest that even a dictator like Bonaparte was powerless to reconcile. 'With the disintegration of small peasant property', Marx writes, 'the state structure erected on it begins to collapse.' In his work he predicts the eventual downfall of Bonaparte, who shortly afterwards became the Emperor Napoleon III, and a sharpening of class conflict between bourgeoisie and proletariat as they battle for state power. The Second Empire lasted until the Emperor was captured in 1870 in the Franco-Prussian War (*Surveys* 238–47).

Marx portrays the insurrectionary Paris Commune of 1871 as the direct antithesis to the Second Empire. In his *The Civil War in France* of the same year he presents the Commune as a movement towards the 'social republic' which is to supersede class rule altogether. His own account is an idealized version of this 'vague aspiration' with much contradictory detail omitted in order to make plain what the Commune exposed. Certain political initiatives interest him a great deal, and his presentation of an idealized Commune gives us an insight into the transitional forms of power in society that he associates with the establishment 'through long struggles' of **communism**.

According to Marx, the Paris Commune was formed of municipal councillors, chosen by universal manhood suffrage. They were to be responsible to the electorate, and revocable by them if its mandated instructions were not obeyed. Such representative institutions were to be generalized across France in a hierarchy of local and district communes, each sending representatives to a higher body culminating in a national one handling the 'few but important' functions of 'central government'.

In Marx's idealized commune all representatives and officials were to be paid working-class wages, the people were to be armed, the standing army was to be abolished and the police were to be responsible to the Commune. The church was to be disestablished, educational institutions were to be opened freely to all, and magistrates and judges were to be made elective, responsible and revocable. This was the political form, according to Marx, under which labour would be emancipated and **exploitation** abolished. With labour emancipated, he writes, every person becomes a worker and 'productive labour ceases to be a class attribute'.

More specifically, he refers to 'co-operative societies' which could 'regulate national production upon a common plan'. This presupposes the abolition of the 'class property which makes the labour of the many the wealth of the few'. Put more starkly this is the 'expropriation of the expropriators'. Co-operative production, guaranteed and co-ordinated by the representative institutions of the Commune, would put an end, so he opines, 'to the constant anarchy and periodical convulsions which are the fatality of capitalist production'. This vision of the Commune, he concludes, is 'possible communism' (*First International* 208–14).

Having defined state power in the *Communist Manifesto* as an instrument by which one class oppresses another, Marx could appropriately use the term 'state' in *The Civil War in France* for proletarian rule as it revolutionizes the economic and administrative structures of society. To accomplish this **revolution** the interests of non-proletarian classes, especially the bourgeoisie, would have to be violated. He uses words such as 'despotic' or 'dictatorship' in his *Critique of the Gotha Programme* of 1875 to characterize a period of working-class rule preceding the introduction of classless society (*First International* 355).

Marx's writings on the Paris Commune indicate the kind of administrative institutions he thinks appropriate in a transition to communist society. They tell us how those arrangements differ from the state as we know it in class-divided societies. Interestingly for Marx the armed working class seems to be quite compatible with the representative institutions and democratic decision-making he sketches in his works.

Conflicts in communist society are never explicitly ruled out by Marx, indeed the possibility that they could exist is confirmed by an implicit continuity between the democratic institutions of the transitional period and communism itself as an organization of freely associated workers. In his view communism is not anarchy, but communist administration after the revolution is not a 'state'. This is because the productive system is egalitarian and social classes do not arise.

FURTHER READING

A Marx Dictionary

alienation	exploitation
base and superstructure	labour
capitalism	mode of production
class	revolution
communism	

Marx's writings

Early Writings, 'On the Jewish Question', especially pp. 220–2, 233–4; 'Economic and Philosophical Manuscripts', especially pp. 424–8

First International, 'Civil War in France', especially pp. 206–21; 'Critique of the Gotha Programme', especially pp. 353–9

Revolutions, 'Communist Manifesto', pp. 79–87

Surveys, 'Eighteenth Brumaire', especially pp. 234–49

Secondary sources

Avineri (1970), especially chapters 1, 2, 7, 8

Carver (1982), especially chapter 4

Giddens (1981), especially chapters 8–9

Giddens (1985), especially chapters 1–6

Gilbert (1981), especially part 3

Maguire (1972), especially chapters 1–2

Maguire (1978), especially chapters 1, 7

Mepham (1981), especially chapters 3, 4, 6

Nove (1985), especially parts 1, 5

Suchting (1983), especially chapters 15, 21

value

A term Marx adopts and redefines for his work on **capitalism**. In his view the **alienation** and **exploitation** that characterize the modern bourgeois **mode of production** arise from the system of market relations through which goods are produced and exchanged. Market relations presuppose private ownership of productive resources and articles of consumption. Those goods are produced for the market and traded there for money. Money is the standard whereby they are priced for exchange and the medium through which their values are realized as cash or units of account.

Two questions that have long puzzled economists are how a system of market values works overall and why particular values are established. In ancient Greece Aristotle proposed a distinction between value-in-use and value-in-exchange that has been the foundation for most analyses of value itself, including Marx's. His work on use-value and exchange-value in the opening pages of *Capital*, volume 1, of 1867, underpins his theory of the **fetishism of commodities**. More particularly his theory of value forms the basis for the theory of surplus-value from which he deduces tendencies in capitalism towards high levels of unemployment, economic crises and proletarian **revolution**.

Using terms derived from traditional scholastic philosophy, Marx argues that commodities – useful objects produced for exchange on the market – 'may be looked at from the two points of view of quality and quantity'. On the qualitative side a useful thing is a whole composed of many properties. Discovering those properties and hence the manifold uses of things is the work of history. He regards the material production of useful things through human history as the fundamental presupposition of social **science**.

'The usefulness of a thing', Marx writes, 'makes it a use-value', a definition that has little meaning without the contrasting term 'exchange-value'. Marx claims that exchange-value appears to express a quantitative relation, 'the proportion, in which use-values of one kind exchange for use-values of another kind'.

Use-value and exchange-value are contrasted by Marx as follows:

1 Use-values are founded on the qualities or properties of objects and have no existence apart from those physical characteristics, though the particular utility of particular properties is something that is socially devised throughout history. Quantitatively use-values can only be measured as aggregations of identical objects, using socially devised standards, e.g. yards of linen.

2 Exchange-value is a quantitative relation between use-values of different sorts irrespective of their physical properties. It is assigned in social organizations of a certain historical type, namely commodity-producing societies. Exchange-values appear to change constantly, as the quantitative relation between use-values in exchange alters with time and circumstance.

3 Use-values are realized in use or consumption, where the material properties of the object and the needs of the particular consumer are paramount. Exchange-value expresses a relation between use-values that is neutral with respect to their different material properties and to the particular needs of particular individuals. This is because in taking account of exchange-value individuals act as traders, rather than consumers, and exchange goods to accumulate value.

4 Use-value is a social necessity, insofar as it is another name for utility. Exchange-value is a social construction peculiar to only one sort of society, so it could be dispensed with if society were organized differently. Use-values constitute 'the material content of wealth, whatever its social form may be'. In societies where 'the capitalist mode of production prevails', the form which wealth assumes is that of an 'immense accumulation of commodities'. Commodities are use-values which, in relation to each other, bear a value-in-exchange (*Capital* 125–31).

On the market the exchange-values of commodities appear in money-terms as prices. As money is accepted in payment and then spent on further goods, the exchange-values of commodities as expressed in money are resolved by Marx (who follows Aristotle) into equations of one commodity for certain proportions of another. However complicated the chain of buyers and sellers and however varied the commodities they exchange, this fundamental equation expresses the worth of one commodity in terms of another.

Thus for Marx the equality of any two different commodities as exchange-values is always an equation of the type '5 beds = 1 house', the example given by Aristotle and cited in *Capital*, volume 1. Marx expresses this view when he states that 'a given commodity, a quarter of wheat for example, is exchanged for x boot polish, y silk or z gold, etc.' Exchange-value 'appears first of all as the quantitative relation, the proportion in which use-values of one kind exchange for use-values of another kind' (*Capital* 126–7, 151).

Exchange-value for Marx is not founded on the preferences of individual consumers that find expression in money-terms, as they make monetary sacrifices to satisfy needs. Rather the equation of commodity for commodity is abstracted from the market process, which admittedly involves consumers and money, because it expresses the intrinsic equality in commodities that enables individuals to use money to value useful goods in the first place.

For Marx money itself is a commodity, such as precious metal weighed out or coined, and paper money and credit are merely token representations of such a commodity acting the role of measure of value and standard of price. His resolution of exchange-value into a fundamental equation of commodity-for-commodity excludes a defining role for money as exclusive measure of worth.

Thus Marx's concept of market exchange is based on a reduction of monetary transactions to equations between commodities of different types, and on a deduction that there can be no exchange without equality, no equality without commensurability and no true commensurability without some common quality or substance on both sides of the equation.

Aristotle could see no such quality or substance that would

render beds and houses commensurable, and so he concluded that the money-valuations which seem to make commodities commensurable and therefore equalizable were mere makeshift arrangements that served for practical purposes. Marx, however, argues that there is a homogeneous element or common substance in commodities equated in money-exchanges. Thus for him the concept of value is the way in which the real equality of commodities as commensurable products finds expression in society (*Capital* 151–2).

In considering commodities as values-in-exchange Marx argues that their particular physical properties or use-values are disregarded, as commodities are in principle exchangeable indiscriminately as values. Similarly the different concrete forms of labour (e.g. spinning, wood-working) which made the commodities are also disregarded. The common substance in commodities must be 'human labour in the abstract', 'human labour-power expended without regard to the form of its expenditure', 'equal human labour', 'the expenditure of identical human labour-power'.

This expenditure of abstract labour-power is measured in socially average units, derived from a conception of the total labour-power of society as a single homogeneous mass. This mass is said to be divisible into individual units from which a notional average unit can theoretically be constructed. Only so many of those units as are necessary to produce a use-value under normal conditions of production in a given society actually count towards the value of an article.

Marx's 'law of value' summarizes certain proportional relationships between value and labour-time, and in that way he defines the productivity of labour.

What exclusively determines the magnitude of the value of any article is therefore the amount of labour socially necessary, or the labour-time socially necessary for its production. The individual commodity counts here only as an average sample of its kind. Commodities which contain equal quantities of labour, or which can be produced in the same time, have therefore the same value. The value of a commodity is related to the value of any other commodity as the labour-time necessary for the production of the one is related to the labour-time necessary for the production of the other.

In general, the greater the productivity of labour, the less the labour-time required to produce an article, the less the mass of labour crystallized in that article, and the less its value. Inversely, the less the productivity of labour, the greater the labour-time necessary to produce an article, and the greater its value. The value of a commodity, therefore, varies directly as the quantity, and inversely as the productivity, of the labour which finds its realization within the commodity (*Capital* 128–37).

Having penetrated the appearance of exchange-value as merely monetary and having established the simplest value-relation as that of one commodity of any kind to another of a different kind, Marx aims to explain the apparently common-place economic phenomena of commodity-producing societies more satisfactorily than was previously the case.

For Marx prices are a deduction from the simple equality in commodity-exchange with which he began, and his derivation is sound, given his premisses. Those premisses exclude money-value and consumer preference as a sufficient explanation for market relations in which useful goods are valued in terms of money and traded for it. That exclusion is highly debatable, not least because it forces him to further exclusions in defining what is properly a commodity.

Marx's model for the commodity is the reproducible labour-product, and it is from the exchange of those objects against each other that he derives his theory of value. A commodity must be useful, he says, though useful things which are not labour-products cannot be commodities, even if, like land, they commonly have a price. Prices assigned to unique objects, such as works of art, or to non-material rights or interests, are also not allowed to disturb his derivation of value from the material production of the general run of goods (*Capital* 131).

While Marx's theory of value is well known, at least in outline, his real purpose in tackling the subject is often somewhat obscured by the intricacies of his analysis and by later critical commentaries. Though the theory of value serves to explain what money is, and how commodities can be valued in exchange, his real interest is in accounting for profits and the accumulation of capital.

Marx tries to solve an apparent paradox in economic theory: how can profits or a surplus-value arise at all, when market exchange allows the *equalization* of commodities according to a standard of value? Does profit arise only when equals are not exchanged for equals? If so, the accumulation of a surplus would be a result of 'cheating', and he argues that throughout the system of exchange such cheating would be evened out over time. Therefore no surplus could ever arise within the system as a whole, although individual 'cheats' might have some success.

At the same time 'using money to make money' is a well-known phenomenon in commodity-producing societies, and Marx comments that this is the characteristic form of capital accumulation. He claims that this accumulation is a process of quantitative increase towards absolute wealth, rather than a qualitative satisfaction of needs that are limited by nature. Thus in his terms capital accumulation is a particular type of endless value-circulation, a circuit in which the quantity of value represented in a sum of money returns to its owner with a profit or excess which he calls surplus-value (*Capital* 247–69).

Through his theory of surplus-value Marx aims to solve the apparent paradox of the formation of profit from the exchange of equal values that he sees as the basis of market relations. His solution is that human labour-power has a peculiar property. It can create new value in excess of its own.

The value of labour-power is the socially necessary labour-time required to raise, train and sustain the labourer. This is because labour-power is a commodity, and for Marx the value of any commodity is determined by the socially necessary labour-time required for its production.

When the capitalist offers a subsistence wage in exchange for a worker's labour-power, equals are exchanged for equals in value-terms. Profit arises, not through an unequal exchange of values, but because in expending their labour-power workers first create commodities with a value equal to their subsistence wage, which the capitalist pays or recoups when those commodities are sold. Then workers create more commodities with a further value in excess of their subsistence wage as they continue working. This surplus labour-time or surplus-value accrues to capitalists as a **class**, rather than to workers. Their exploitation arises because the surplus-value is invested or consumed by capitalists independently of the workers who performed the labour.

Marx's argument is not that workers should have the full product of their labour as wages, but that the exchange of labour-power at its value allows a surplus to accrue to capitalists. Indeed such an exchange would have little point for a capitalist unless that were the motive.

The theory of surplus-value enables Marx to argue that the rate of exploitation of workers is often far in excess of the rate of profit in many capitalist firms, because the surplus-value created in the production process is more properly compared to the expenditure on wages or 'variable capital' alone, rather than to variable and 'constant capital' added together. Constant capital, according to Marx, refers to means of production and raw materials, i.e. factors of production other than labour, rent or interest. In his view profits do not arise from machines and raw materials, but only from 'living' or 'fluid' labour by definition, so the value represented in the 'congealed', 'dead' or 'objectified' labour of constant capital is merely transferred as those goods are used up in producing the commodities which the capitalist can offer for sale. Thus the capitalists' profit does not arise from the total capital tied up in a firm, but only from the portion expended on wages. Relative to wages surplus-value is necessarily a much larger percentage than it is relative to total capital. Real rates of exploitation, Marx argues, may be more than 100 per cent (*Capital* 270–339).

Marx's theory of surplus-value ascribes to human labour the mysterious power to expend more energy as 'abstract labour' than is required in equivalent terms to reproduce it. This enables him to examine production, laying bare the processes by which the drive for profit influences the conditions of work that some human beings impose on others.

Marx's theory of surplus-value implies that the working day in capitalist enterprises can be divided into two parts, one portion in which the workers' labour, as the expenditure of socially necessary labour-time, creates value equal to wages, and a further portion in which the worker creates additional value, which is appropriated by the capitalist as a surplus over wage-costs. Capitalism incorporates a 'werewolf-like hunger for surplus labour', Marx argues, and the individual capitalist tries to make the working day as long as possible. Hence in the capitalist economic system there is an inevitable struggle between classes over the norm for the length of the working day.

In his chapter 'The Working Day' in *Capital*, volume 1, Marx uses British parliamentary reports and contemporary journalism to document the way that workers, especially women and children, were made to work past all physical and moral limits in certain industries and enterprises, especially mining and textile manufacture. 'Capital therefore takes no account of the health and the length of life of the worker', he writes, 'unless society forces it to do so.' He concludes that 'the workers have to put their heads together and, as a class, compel the passing of a law, an all-powerful social barrier by which they can be prevented from selling themselves and their families into slavery and death by voluntary contract with capital' (*Capital* 340–416).

But lengthening the working day is not the only way in which capitalists can increase surplus-value. The amount of time the worker needs to create value equal to wages can vary, and the lengths of the two portions of the working day can thus alter relative to each other. Marx calls an increase in surplus-value arising from a lengthening of the working day an increase in 'absolute surplus-value'. But an increase in surplus-value arising from a shortening of the labour-time necessary to cover wages he calls an increase in 'relative surplus-value'.

Any increase in the productivity of labour, whereby more goods are produced with the same expenditure of labour-power, causes commodities to cheapen in value-terms. Because this happens to the subsistence commodities which workers buy, the value required to maintain and reproduce the working class through the payment of wages will gradually fall over time. Workers will need to labour less in order to earn a subsistence package of goods, since the goods themselves will require less labour to produce. Marx concludes that capital 'has an immanent drive, and a constant tendency, towards increasing the productivity of labour, in order to cheapen commodities and, by cheapening commodities, to cheapen the worker' (*Capital* 417–38).

Marx argues that few of the benefits of the increased productivity of labour are passed on to workers, because capitalists necessarily strive to keep wages at subsistence. The primary way that the productivity of labour is increased is through the introduction of co-operation, manufacture and large-scale machinery into industry, enabling workers to produce a very high output of goods for each unit of labour-power expended.

New technology is introduced, Marx theorizes, when it is cheaper to buy and run than human labour doing the same tasks. Overall he expects the cost of machines in value-terms to be lower than the cost of maintaining and reproducing human beings at subsistence, so the capitalist system tends to make workers redundant. Moreover as industry is mechanized it becomes easier for capitalists to increase the intensity of labour by speeding up assembly lines, breaking up work-processes into smaller, more repetitious phases and generally making human beings into appendages of machines. While recognizing the enormous increase in productivity that the introduction of machinery makes possible, Marx also emphasizes the human cost and draws dramatic conclusions concerning the way that those increases in productivity are achieved.

In the factory code, the capitalist formulates his autocratic power over his workers like a private legislator, and purely as an emanation of his own will, unaccompanied by either that division of responsibility otherwise so much approved of by the bourgeoisie, or the still more approved representative system. This code is merely the capitalist caricature of the social regulation of the labour process which becomes necessary in co-operation on a large scale and in the employment in common of instruments of labour, and especially of machinery. The overseer's book of penalties replaces the slave-driver's lash. All punishments naturally resolve themselves into fines and deduction from wages, and the law-giving talent of the factory Lycurgus so arranges matters that a violation of his laws is, if possible, more profitable to him than the keeping of them (*Capital* 549–50).

Thus Marx's theory of surplus-value, and his whole approach to the capitalist system, turns on his claim that the intensity of labour, its productivity and the length of the working day all may vary. Because in Marx's view capitalist production is by its very essence the production of surplus-value, individual capitalists characteristically seek to lengthen the working day and to increase the productivity and intensity of labour, subjecting workers to subsistence wages or worse and to brutal, machine-driven processes of production. By making labour the sole source of value, and treating the capitalists' role in the market as non-productive, Marx's analysis shows how capitalists strive to cut costs at the expense of workers (*Capital* 439–654).

However, the theory of surplus-value rests on Marx's view that in buying labour-time the capitalist acquires the monetary value as well as the goods that labour-time creates. Some of that monetary value is returned to workers as wages, while the rest is surplus, and the capitalist strives to increase this excess over production costs in the ways described.

It may be argued that Marx has telescoped two exchanges into one. While the capitalist exchanges wages for labour-power and acquires the goods produced, those goods must then be exchanged on the market for money. Marx telescopes two exchanges – wages for products and products for money – into one exchange – value for surplus-value. This may call into question some of his conclusions about the capitalist system. If the second exchange is logically separate from the first his theory lacks the crucial connecting link between surplus-value and 'living' labour-time that allows him to deduce a declining rate of profit and worsening economic crises within the capitalist system as a whole.

FURTHER READING

A Marx Dictionary
alienation
capitalism
class
exploitation

fetishism of commodities
labour
revolution
science

Marx's writings
Capital, especially pp. 125–31, 247–69, 643–54

Secondary sources
Brewer (1984), especially chapters 1–15
Carver (1982), especially chapter 6
Cleaver (1979), especially chapters III, V
Fine (1975), especially chapters 2–3
Lichtenstein (1983), especially parts V–VI
Suchting (1983), especially chapters 6–10
Walton and Gamble (1972), especially chapter 6

Bibliographical Essay

In this essay I have used **bold-face** type to indicate books listed in the bibliography, where full details of publication may be found.

MARX'S WRITINGS

I have chosen the 'Marx Library' paperback edition for quoted texts and references in *A Marx Dictionary*. Although the 'Marx Library' is not the most competitively priced collection it has virtues for the student that outweigh this disadvantage. It presents a wide variety of Marx's works complete, rather than as excerpts, and includes manuscript materials.

The volumes in the 'Marx Library' have individual titles and are available separately. **Early Writings** includes the *Economic and Philosophical Manuscripts* written in 1844, the manuscript theses *Concerning Feuerbach* written in 1845, and the published 'Preface' of 1859 to *A Contribution to the Critique of Political Economy*. **The Revolutions of 1848** contains the published *Communist Manifesto* of 1848 and a selection of journalism from the revolutionary period. **Surveys from Exile** includes *The Class Struggles in France* published in 1850, *The Eighteenth Brumaire of Louis Bonaparte* published in 1852 and some of the other political journalism of the 1850s. **The First International and After** contains *The Civil War in France* published in 1871, the manuscript *Critique of the Gotha Programme* written in 1875 and many documents relating to the International Working Men's Association or 'First International' which Marx helped to found in 1864. The **Grundrisse** manuscripts written in 1857–8 and **Capital**, volume 1, published in 1867, are an integral part of the collection, and all the volumes contain informative introductions.

The nearest rival to the 'Marx Library' is the Lawrence & Wishart/International Publishers *Selected Works* by Karl Marx and Frederick Engels in a one-volume edition, together with Marx's *Capital*, volume 1, from the same publishers. These books lack interesting modern introductions, and many important works are omitted, such as the *Economic and Philosophical Manuscripts*, *The Class Struggles in France* and many of the letters, articles and documents included in the 'Marx Library'. Some of those works are available in separate editions from Lawrence & Wishart/International Publishers or in their *Selected Works* in three volumes, but they are sometimes hard to obtain.

Both the 'Marx Library' and the Lawrence & Wishart/International Publishers one-volume *Selected Works* omit *The German Ideology*, an important manuscript work of 1845 and 1846, presumably because it is too rambling to be published complete in a student edition. This is a shame, as Part One of the work is not excessively long, and there is indeed a Lawrence & Wishart/International Publishers version of this section. Moreover *The German Ideology* is perhaps the one work that actually lends itself to excerpting without significant loss, since the manuscript materials are so defective, unfinished and jumbled that the book, especially Part One, is almost a set of excerpts anyway.

There are many popular collections of Marx's writings, which I do not recommend, that make extensive use of excerpts. Note particularly that the 'Karl Marx Library' edited by Saul K. Padover is not the same as the recommended 'Marx Library' discussed above. I think that the student gains from reading a work as a whole and getting the feel of it, even if that whole work is an unfinished one or one unedited by Marx. Reading works complete makes it easier to consider the intended audience, and to take that into account when interpreting his ideas. Skilful editors can make up for this when presenting excerpts, and reading a work whole by no means guarantees a better response from students or more cogent interpretations. Even so, I think the balance tips away from excerpts and towards reading Marx's works complete, and the 'Marx Library' takes this approach.

The large-scale *Collected Works* by Karl Marx and Frederick Engels from Lawrence & Wishart/International Publishers has been in progress since 1975. Eventually the 50 volumes or so will cover all works of Marx and Engels published in their lifetimes, many manuscripts and all their letters. This English-language collection is based on the definitive scholarly edition begun in 1972 by Dietz Verlag of East Berlin. Their 100-volume set (known as the new MEGA), will eventually comprise all materials by Marx and Engels in the original languages with textual variants, as well as relevant letters from third parties. For further publication details and additional reference works, see my 'Guide to Further Reading' in Isaiah Berlin, *Karl Marx*, 4th edn (Oxford and New York: Oxford University Press, 1978; updated for subsequent reprints). The Guide also lists a considerable amount of secondary literature on Marx, including biographies, so in the comments which follow I shall confine myself to discussing the works recommended in *A Marx Dictionary*.

SECONDARY SOURCES

For an introduction to Marx's work I recommend **Suchting (1983)**, **Wood (1981)** and **Carver (1982)**. Suchting's book is probably the best short study in a chronological framework and it gives considerable emphasis to the development of Marx's critical work on capitalist society culminating in *Capital*, volume 1. Some biographical material and details of Marx's own political involvements are included.

Wood's volume is part of a series 'The Arguments of the Philosophers', and the topical arrangement of his study reflects this concern. His book includes major sections on alienation, materialism and dialectic, and particular contributions to two current debates – one on the nature of historical explanation and the other on Marx's relationship to morality and justice. The former raises questions concerning technological determinism and the latter explores the difficulties of reconciling Marx's advocacy of communist revolution with his apparent dismissal of morality as merely ideological. Further specialist studies on those areas are considered below.

Carver presents Marx's social theory to the student by explaining Marx's own 'guiding principle', which appears in the 'Preface' to *A Contribution to the Critique of Political Economy*. Marx summarized his views on society and social change in an autobiographical context which Carver details. Marx's generalizations are then interpreted, assessed and related to his earlier and later works, in particular *Capital*, volume 1. Carver questions the traditional distinction between Marx's 'theory of history' and his 'economics' of capitalist society by introducing a new unifying category 'production theory of society and social change'. This is derived from a close reading of Marx's own account of his lifework.

Avineri (1970) is a classic scholarly study which focused academic attention on Marx's early writings and made plausible a view of Marx quite different from the one that figured in traditional Marxist accounts. The work is especially controversial on Marx's politics but can be recommended for a detailed examination of his early confrontation with Hegel.

Walton and Gamble (1972) trace the development of Marx's theory from the general category 'alienation' to the more specific terms of *Capital*, volume 1, emphasizing the continuity and increasing specificity of Marx's work. The authors explore his preoccupation with the distribution of wealth and power which derive from the economic structure of society. The book may be hard to find, but it has solid virtues as an introduction to the main elements of Marx's social theory.

Two studies of Marx's politics deserve a recommendation, if only as a partial corrective to treatments of the theoretical aspects of his work. Though academic authors usually remind readers that Marx worked in a highly political context and had a highly political view of his own activities as a theorist, the studies of Marx that focus on his theoretical work inevitably resort to summary and overview of his actual political involvements. By contrast **Gilbert (1981)** is a controversial, historically detailed reconstruction of Marx's political activity, though almost all of the book is concerned with the years up to 1853. **Maguire (1978)** is a more topical discussion of various themes, such as revolution, state and political action that arise in Marx's work.

Perhaps because of Marx's reticence on the subject of socialism and communism there is little to recommend in terms of specific studies of future society beyond the introductory works on Marx mentioned above. **Mepham (1981)** contains a number of essays on current topics in social and political philosophy, such as community and equality, written by different authors who take Marx's work as a point of departure. In **Nove (1985)** the author explores a conception of feasible socialism which he introduces with critical reference to Marx. Nove attempts to work out some of the practicalities of industrial production that Marx was inclined to leave to others.

Marx's generalizations concerning modes of production, forces and relations of production, base and superstructure and revolution became known as his 'interpretation' or 'theory of history'. For an overview of Marx as a theorist of history, see **Rader (1979)**, where the author's aim is exposition rather than criticism.

Cohen (1978) is a self-confessed defence of Marx's 'theory of history', and the author argues that Marx's generalizations represent a version of technological determinism which can be expounded using the methods of modern analytical philosophy. This study has sparked a large critical literature from other scholars. Cohen has recently had some doubts concerning the validity of the 'theory of history', though none yet concerning the accuracy with which he has interpreted Marx. **Shaw (1978)** is a similar but briefer work interpreting Marx as a technological determinist.

Giddens (1981) and **Giddens (1985)** are an altogether more exploratory critique of Marx's social theory. The author maps the way that Marx might be interpreted, outlines the utility of his views and details where he is misleading or inadequate in explaining the way that social structures function and change.

On pre-capitalist societies and the way that Marx's insights can be critically applied, I recommend **Bloch (1984)**. In that work there is an exceptionally interesting account of the way that Marx anticipated modern scientific anthropology. **Sawer (1977)** is the standard study of Marx's concept of the Asisatic mode of production, including his application of it in research, further use of the concept by Marxists and a critical assessment.

Turner (1978) is an excellent short work on the way that sociologists and anthropologists, inspired by Marx's work on capitalism, colonialism and the general structure of human society, have confronted Orientalism – a way of interpreting the history and politics of the Middle East that relies on culture, especially Islamic, as an explanatory category. Turner argues that Marxists have in some cases unwittingly absorbed the very approach to which Marx's work is sharply contrasting.

Wallerstein (1983) outlines the transition from pre-capitalist societies to capitalism. He indicates the features that make one type of society different from another and assesses the results achieved under capitalism compared with other systems.

Fine (1975) and **Brewer (1984)** are two excellent short introductions to Marx's work in *Capital*, volume 1, and to issues raised in volumes 2 and 3. Both books are by economists who concentrate on Marx's conception of the capitalist economy, in particular his theory of production and the contrast between it and the economic theories that have developed since his time. Neither is a commentary on Marx's actual text. Rather the strength of the two is the way that his overall theory of capitalism as a functioning economic system is clearly presented.

Cleaver (1979) offers a commentary on chapter 1 of *Capital*, volume 1, detailing various ways that the work has been read within the Marxist tradition and relating Marx's propositions to contemporary politics. The relation between Marx's work on value and recent work in economics is lucidly detailed in **Lichtenstein (1983)**, and from there the student can progress to three more specialized studies that assess Marx's theory of exploitation: **Hodgson (1982)**, **Roemer (1982)** and **Weeks (1981)**.

Marx's concept of alienation arises in his *Economic and Philosophical Manuscripts* of 1844 and is dealt with there at greatest length. Those manuscripts and other works of the period are analysed in detail in **Maguire (1972)**. The concept of alienation is expounded and related to Marx's later work in **Mészáros (1972)** and **Ollman (1976)**.

Marx's method of conceptual analysis, particularly as applied to economic concepts, is considered in **Sayer (1979)**. The definition and function of a dialectic within this method is debated in the contributions to **Norman (1980)** and **Mepham (1979a)**. **Callinicos (1983)** and **Ruben (1979)** deal with the related issues of materialism and science, as do the contributors to **Mepham (1979b)**.

The relation of science to ideology, as Marx conceived them, is explored in the essays in **Mepham (1979c)**. **McCarney (1980)** and **Parekh (1982)** present interpretations of Marx's concept of ideology that conflict sharply over the relationship of ideology to class interest, morality and truth.

I have chosen these secondary works for their scholarly qualities, accessibility to students and lively discussion. They include many views diametrically opposed to mine, and I hope that students will find these contrasts stimulating.

Bibliography

MARX'S WRITINGS

Capital   Karl Marx, *Capital*, vol. 1, tr. Ben Fowkes, 'Marx Library', Harmondsworth and London: Penguin Books and New Left Review, 1976; New York: Random House/Vintage and Monthly Review, 1977.

Early Writings   Karl Marx, *Early Writings*, tr. Rodney Livingstone and Gregor Benton, 'Marx Library', Harmondsworth and London: Penguin Books and New Left Review; New York: Random House/Vintage and Monthly Review; 1975.

First International   Karl Marx, *Political Writings*, vol. 3: *The First International and After*, ed. David Fernbach, 'Marx Library', Harmondsworth and London: Penguin Books and New Left Review; New York: Random House/Vintage and Monthly Review; 1974.

Grundrisse   Karl Marx, *Grundrisse*, tr. Martin Nicolaus, 'Marx Library', Harmondsworth and London: Penguin Books and New Left Review; New York: Random House/Vintage and Monthly Review; 1974.

Revolutions   Karl Marx, Political Writings, vol. 1: *The Revolutions of 1848*, ed. David Fernbach, 'Marx Library', Harmondsworth and London: Penguin Books and New Left Review, 1973; New York: Random House/Vintage and Monthly Review, 1974.

Surveys   Karl Marx, *Political Writings*, vol. 2: *Surveys from Exile*, ed. David Fernbach, 'Marx Library', Harmondsworth and London: Penguin Books and New Left Review, 1973; New York: Random House/Vintage and Monthly Review, 1974.

SECONDARY SOURCES

Avineri (1970)   Shlomo Avineri, *The Social and Political Thought of Karl Marx*, London and New York: Cambridge University Press.

Bloch (1984)   Maurice Bloch, *Marxism and Anthropology*, Oxford and New York: Oxford University Press.

Brewer (1984)   Anthony Brewer, *A Guide to Marx's 'Capital'*, London and New York: Cambridge University Press.

Callinicos (1983)   Alex Callinicos, *Marxism and Philosophy*, Oxford and New York: Oxford University Press.

Carver (1982)   Terrell Carver, *Marx's Social Theory*, Oxford and New York: Oxford University Press.

Cleaver (1979)   Harry Cleaver, *Reading 'Capital' Politically*, Brighton: Harvester Press; Austin: University of Texas Press.

Cohen (1978)   G.A. Cohen, *Karl Marx's Theory of History: A Defence*, Oxford: Oxford University Press; Princeton, N.J.: Princeton University Press.

Fine (1975)   Ben Fine, *Marx's 'Capital'*, London: Macmillan.

Giddens (1981)   Anthony Giddens, *A Contemporary Critique of Historical Materialism*, vol. 1: *Power, Property and the State*, London: Macmillan; Berkeley: University of California Press.

Giddens (1985)   Anthony Giddens, *A Contemporary Critique of Historical Materialism*, vol. 2: *The Nation-state and Violence*, Cambridge: Polity; Berkeley: University of California Press; 1985.

Gilbert (1981)   Alan Gilbert, *Marx's Politics*, Oxford: Martin Robertson; Rutgers, N.J.: Rutgers University Press.

Hodgson (1982)   Geoff Hodgson, *Capitalism, Value and Exploitation*, Oxford: Martin Robertson.

Lichtenstein (1983)   P.M. Lichtenstein, *An Introduction to Post-Keynesian and Marxian Theories of Value and Price*, London: Macmillan; Armonk, N.Y.: M.E. Sharpe.

McCarney (1980)   Joe McCarney, *The Real World of Ideology*, Brighton: Harvester Press; New York: Humanities Press.

Maguire (1972)   John [M.] Maguire, *Marx's Paris Writings: An Analysis*, Dublin and London: Gill and Macmillan; New York: Barnes and Noble.

Maguire (1978)   John M. Maguire, *Marx's Theory of Politics*,

Cambridge and New York: Cambridge University Press.

Mepham (1979a) John Mepham and David-Hillel Ruben (eds), *Issues in Marxist Philosophy*, vol. 1: *Dialectics and Method*, Brighton: Harvester Press; New York: Humanities Press.

Mepham (1979b) John Mepham and David-Hillel Ruben (eds), *Issues in Marxist Philosophy*, vol. 2: *Materialism*, Brighton: Harvester Press; New York: Humanities Press.

Mepham (1979c) John Mepham and David-Hillel Ruben (eds), *Issues in Marxist Philosophy*, vol. 3: *Epistemology, Science, Ideology*, Brighton: Harvester Press; New York: Humanities Press.

Mepham (1981) John Mepham and David-Hillel Ruben (eds), *Issues in Marxist Philosophy*, vol. 4: *Social and Political Philosophy*, Brighton: Harvester Press; New York: Humanities Press.

Mészáros (1972) István Mészáros, *Alienation: Marx's Conception of Man in Capitalist Society*, 3rd edn, London: Merlin Press; New York: Harper & Row.

Norman (1980) Richard Norman and Sean Sayers, *Hegel, Marx and Dialectic: A Debate*, Brighton: Harvester Press; New York: Humanities Press.

Nove (1985) Alec Nove, *The Economics of Feasible Socialism*, London and Boston, Mass.: George Allen & Unwin.

Ollman (1976) Bertell Ollman, *Alienation: Marx's Conception of Man in Capitalist Society*, 2nd edn, London and New York: Cambridge University Press.

Parekh (1982) Bhikhu Parekh, *Marx's Theory of Ideology*, London: Croom Helm; Baltimore, Md.: Johns Hopkins University Press.

Rader (1979) Melvin Rader, *Karl Marx's Theory of History*, Oxford and New York: Oxford University Press.

Roemer (1982) John E. Roemer, *A General Theory of Exploitation and Class*, Cambridge, Mass.: Harvard University Press.

Ruben (1979) David Hillel-Ruben, *Marxism and Materialism: A Study in the Marxist Theory of Knowledge*, 2nd edn, Brighton: Harvester Press; New York: Humanities Press.

Sawer (1977) Marian Sawer, *Marxism and the Question of the Asiatic Mode of Production*, The Hague: Martinus Nijhoff.

Sayer (1979) Derek Sayer, *Marx's Method*, Brighton: Harvester Press; New York: Humanities Press.

Shaw (1978) William H. Shaw, *Marx's Theory of History*,

158 Bibliography

London: Hutchinson; Palo Alto, Calif.: Stanford University Press.

Suchting (1983) W.A. Suchting, *Marx: An Introduction*, Brighton: Harvester Press; New York: New York University Press.

Turner (1978) Bryan S. Turner, *Marx and the End of Orientalism*, London and Boston, Mass.: George Allen & Unwin.

Wallerstein (1983) Immanuel Wallerstein, *Historical Capitalism*, London: New Left Books; New York: Schocken Books.

Walton and Gamble (1972) Paul Walton and Andrew Gamble, *From Alienation to Surplus Value*, London: Sheed and Ward.

Weeks (1981) John Weeks, *Capital and Exploitation*, London: Edward Arnold; Princeton, N.J.: Princeton University Press.

Wood (1981) Allen W. Wood, *Karl Marx*, London and Boston, Mass.: Routledge & Kegan Paul.

Index